Foreword by President

Multi-Cult…

The View from the Two Irelands

EDNA LONGLEY

and

DECLAN KIBERD

Cork University Press

in association with

The Centre for Cross Border Studies, Armagh

First published in 2001 by
Cork University Press
University College
Cork
Ireland

British Library Cataloguing in Publication Data
A CIP catalogue record for this book is available from
the British Library

ISBN 1 85918 311 5

Typeset by Tower Books, Ballincollig, Co. Cork
Printed by Colour Books Ltd, Baldoyle, Dublin

Contents

Foreword

MARY McALEESE
President of Ireland

For anybody studying the theme of multi-culturalism in Ireland, I believe that many important lessons can be learnt from the Good Friday Agreement. It seeks to create an institutional and constitutional framework within which people from both main communities and both main traditions can come together to work for their mutual benefit, without abandoning their basic identities or beliefs. Inspired by universal concepts of reconciliation, equality and parity of esteem, it specifically recognises the 'full and equal legitimacy and worth of the identities, senses of allegiance, and ethos of all sections of the community in Northern Ireland'. It has led to the strengthening of human rights and equality provisions. The importance of respect, understanding and tolerance in relation to linguistic diversity is enshrined in the Agreement.

We all have a tendency to live in our own little enclaves. Most of us grow up in an environment where one cultural or religious influence dominates, often to the exclusion of other outside influences. In Northern Ireland, this is perhaps especially true. I have referred elsewhere to the two separate worlds which side by side, cheek by jowl, have inhabited Northern Ireland, without 'co-habiting' in the modern sense. Two cultures, two identities, inhabiting the same spot but travelling in their hearts towards different destinations.

The Centre for Cross Border Studies, with its independent and academically based research work, should go a long way towards establishing how practical cross border co-operation can be improved. The fact that its pilot phase is being financed by the EU Special Support Programme for Peace and Reconciliation, and that it intends to pursue its studies in a wider European context, is highly significant. Traditionally, as well as more recently, Europe has been home to people of many different cultures already settled in one place, and to those arriving from across borders within Europe, or from further afield, in pursuit of a better life. As a Centre for Cross Border Studies, it is ideally placed to examine these experiences and their implications for Ireland.

Of course, the challenges outlined in the Good Friday Agreement concerning fairness, partnership and equality of opportunities are not restricted to Northern Ireland or to the two mainstream cultures there. Along with the rest of Europe, people south of the border are learning to accommodate change and diversity. We are gradually moving away from the homogeneity and old certainties which have traditionally been the hallmarks of Irish life. We are rapidly becoming one of the wealthier states in the world, as well as a multi-cultural society.

This means that we have to confront new ideas and experiences, and re-examine our old attitudes to the asylum-seeker or economic migrant or any stranger in Irish society. In referring to the fact that in the far-off days of Irish history, cultural hybridity between English colonisers and native Gael was regarded with hostility — 'as two discrepant codes cancelling each out' — Declan Kiberd writes that, 'Humans display a dreadful need to make other people more like them.' We must try and prevent this being an overriding impulse and learn to celebrate difference.

People on the whole island can draw on the deep collective memory of emigration, when men and women from every part of Ireland made their homes around the world, driven abroad by economic or political circumstances; or as in the case of Christian missionaries, by the desire to help other people. The experiences undergone by Irish emigrants throughout the ages, both good and bad, and the ties which still bind us to every corner of the globe, are a huge resource of distilled wisdom and experience which should inform our attitudes and policies. The cross-border dimension will help ensure the widest possible discussion which this theme deserves. One hopes that, in promoting mutual understanding, tolerance and respect for diversity, it will assist the gradual shift from a culture of conflict to a culture of comfortable co-habitation and consensus.

Multi-Culturalism and Northern Ireland: Making Differences Fruitful

EDNA LONGLEY

Introduction

I want to begin with a reminder of what Irish *mono*-culturalism can be like. In October 2000 a conference was held in Kilkenny to celebrate the centenary of Hubert Butler's birth. Butler, whose cultural essays were not properly valued until the 1980s, was an Anglo-Irishman, an Irish nationalist and an Irish Protestant. He was also a translator from the Russian and an expert on the culture and politics of former Yugoslavia. He set Irish affairs in a European context and saw them in a European light. Butler often criticised the 'don't rock the boat' mentality of other southern Irish Protestants. In 1952 he spectacularly rocked the boat when he called attention to certain facts about Archbishop Stepinac of Croatia. Stepinac was then being persecuted by the Communist regime, and the Irish Catholic Church had joined the vocal international protest. Yet Stepinac himself had condoned the violent campaign of Pavelic, Croatia's pro-fascist wartime ruler, to convert Orthodox Serbs to Catholicism. At a meeting in Dublin Butler spoke of this forced conversion and massacre, and the Papal Nuncio walked out. For 'insulting the Nuncio' Butler was widely condemned. He was ostracised in Kilkenny and excluded from the Kilkenny Archaeological Society which he had founded. At the Butler centenary event

Paul Cuddihy, the Mayor of Kilkenny, made a magnificent public apology to his memory.

Hubert Butler was a kind of multi-culturalist martyr. Like-minded people from every Irish background have suffered variations on the same fate. You might be shunned. You might be shot. And, despite the positive symbolism of the Mayor's apology, I suspect that we have not yet arrived at a happy ending. Butler's difficulties in mid twentieth-century Ireland are a warning for the present. He was treated like a heretic, and this exemplifies how religious differences have shaped the structure as well as the content of Irish political differences. Hence the tendency to polarisation rather than argument in Irish intellectual life, too. At its most intense, the liaison between Protestantism and unionism, Catholicism and nationalism, has been consummated in passionate mystiques of blood, soil and heroic death. The unique territorial rivalry and intimacy of the North (a 'frontier-zone' it has been called) potentially fosters these mystiques and imbues politics with a persistent theological ferocity. The contending parties in Northern Ireland qualify as 'ethnic groups' because they define themselves according to religious difference and different historical narratives. The scant tradition of ecumenism between nationalist and unionist ideology means that the 1998 Good Friday Agreement lacks cultural roots. Butler's sin was that he violated the taboo which says — though now less confidently — that Irish Catholics and Protestants should keep to their own boxes, they should not meddle in one another's religious or political business. Even if you do not see yourself in a box, others may put you there and close the lid. It is no coincidence that Butler also violated taboos on intercourse between the unionist North and the Republic (he brought unionist politicians south for public debates). What he wrote of cross-border relations in 1955 explains the need for a Centre for Cross Border Studies in 2001:

> At present there is, south and north of the border an almost unbelievable spiritual stagnation. A dumb, stupid antagonism breaks into an occasional muffled snarl or jeer. Where there is disagreement, there should at least be the stimulus of conflict. It is from challenge and reponse that civilisations have risen in the past. Why are our differences so unfruitful? Here is one reason. Too many people would sooner be silent or untruthful than disloyal to their own side . . . And so there is always a drift towards crisis, a gentle, persistent pressure towards some simple alignment of Good and Evil, Friend and Enemy.

Obstacles to Multi-Culturalism (or Inter-Culturalism)

Hubert Butler's question abides: how can we make our differences fruitful? Cross-border communication has been developed but hardly transformed, at least where unionism is concerned, and Northern Ireland has patented 'dumb, stupid antagonism'. This essay will suggest that multi-culturalism in these islands is indivisible. There can be no such thing as multi-culturalism in one country, or on one side of the border, without reference to the rest of an archipelago whose populations — as countless family histories testify — are so inter-twined. The United Kingdom is itself (conceptually) in flux. The peace process, combined with Scottish and Welsh devolution, has created a volatile 'post-Ukanian' situation — Ukania being Tom Nairn's rather derisive name for the United Kingdom. The Irish Free State was, of course, the first post-Ukanian entity. I prefer 'post-Ukanian' to 'post-colonial', although the terms are not mutually exclusive. But the latter term may blur the specifics of British Isles history and imply too close a parallel between Ireland and, say, India. Independent Ireland's post-Ukanian phase of internal consolidation, whether necessary or not, produced the opposite of a multi-cultural ethos. This particularly applied to cultural ties with Britain. The liberalisation of recent years sits uneasily with unresolved issues which the Good Friday Agreement and closer association with a fractured Northern Ireland have forced to the surface. Thus the Republic too confronts flux and redefinition, even as the Celtic Tiger destabilises its self-understanding from another direction.

British Isles history slots into European history and into Europe's *internal* colonial relations. The Republic's enthusiasm for the EU sometimes gives the impression that southern Ireland only became European thirty years ago when it had finally got over being British. Culturally speaking, both these propositions are doubtful. Ireland has always been caught up in European dynamics (as the Stepinac story shows). The Republic's cultural 'Britishness' continues to evolve. The 'Irish' strand in 'British' culture is becoming more pronounced and more acknowledged. Even Tony Blair is Irish now. He begins his contribution to a recent anthology called *Being Irish* with the statement: 'Ireland is in my blood.' Then he traces a typical migratory move (on his mother's side) from Donegal to Glasgow, and refers accurately to 'the influence of Irish people in almost every facet of British life'. We still await a Taoiseach who will say: 'Britain is in my blood.' Perhaps he/she is more likely to claim transatlantic kin, as with Síle de Valera's and Mary Harney's recent turning away from Europe: the one for nationalist, the other for economic reasons. Not only can the Republic's bearing towards Europe and America appear opportunistic. It masks the state's failure to reflect more deeply on Ireland's cultural whereabouts and cultural differences. This failure is mirrored, of course, by the historical behaviour of Ulster unionism. Current hostility in both jurisdictions to economic immigrants, and to longer-settled communities like the Chinese and Vietnamese, is inseparable from both these failures. Images of the hospitable Irish or friendly Ulster-folk are sentimental. Anti-immigrant and racist feeling should not have been such a shock. It continues the sectarian, exclusivist, conservative and insular attitudes that helped to produce the Troubles. The title of a new book which discloses high rates of anti-immigrant prejudice in the Republic — *Cultivating Pluralism* — sums up a historically neglected task.

Nevertheless, mono-cultural attitudes have been changing more rapidly in the Republic. There exclusivism is directly challenged by pluralism; whereas the North's twin blocs perpetually squeeze the pluralistic centre. But two broad obstacles remain to a fully multi-cultural Ireland. The first is when multi-culturalism is a minimalist goal; the second, when it is not necessarily seen as a desirable or valid goal.

Multi-culturalism as a minimalist principle signifies cultural co-existence rather than cultural exchange. That is, it simply describes a state-ethos which ensures equal treatment for members of diverse groups. Here equity is guaranteed by a Bill of Rights such as that being specially prepared for Northern Ireland. In some circumstances, a minimalist, constitutional multi-culturalism may be enough. Often it does not create too many problems, if small minorities stay in their separate boxes and confine themselves to opening interesting restaurants. The case for multi-cultural minimalism in Northern Ireland is different. A violent conflict, to which issues of discrimination have been integral, requires, in the early stages of its resolution, communal guarantees to the main contending groups. This is where 'parity of esteem' comes in. To Northern Irish Catholics, 'parity of esteem' means long-overdue equal recognition for their modes and emblems of communal self-expression. To unionists, however, the UK state is imperilled if its ceremonial is diluted, its emblems relativised, because they contribute to an unequal environment. The symbolic domain, revealingly, matters most. Hence the row when Sinn Féin ministers objected to union jacks flying on the buildings that house their departments. Hence, too, the extraordinary conflict over the title and badge rather than actuality of the police. In fact, the argument about public symbolism itself symbolises different kinds or degrees of multi-culturalism: discreet state-insignia with no prohibition of other emblems where local communities desire them (already a *fait accompli*); union jacks and tricolours flying side by side; wholly new flags and emblems for a new Northern Ireland.

The Faith and Politics Group, which favours linking the last two options to reflect 'the complex condition of Northern Ireland', nonetheless warns:

> In a contested space governed by a mutual fear-threat relationship parity of esteem language often becomes simply

part of the fight between the two communities. It is used to make claims and demands which others have to fulfil. What we need is a new relationship between the two communities in which, when making claims and demands, they seek to take into account those of the other.

In the longer term 'parity of esteem' could cement the existing blocs. Rather than a transitional *means*, it could become a frozen *end*: a charter for apartheid. It may be important that the Bill of Rights should not name (and thereby limit) the groups whose members' rights it guarantees. The Agreement itself will not necessarily induce a richer multi-culturalism since it follows a 'consociational' model for internal governance. Robin Wilson sums up consociationalism as 'characterised by grand coalition, mutual veto, proportionality (such as in "the spoils of office") and the autonomy of different segments from one another'. Noting its divisive consequences in Belgium and elsewhere, Wilson criticises consociationalism because 'identities are perceived in an essentialist fashion, separation is preferred to integration, and politics is perceived as a process confined to élite deal-makers best subject to minimum popular pressure'. Thus consociational government tends to reinforce ethnic mono-culturalism (Flemings and Walloons) rather than open up civic space for cultural exchange. Such exchange might include asking whether groups deserve parity of *dis*esteem.

Yet is it the ethnic buzz that most Northern Irish people desire? And are they, perhaps, in tune with the times if they will accept only a minimal multi-culturalism or none at all? Michael Ignatieff worryingly argues that, 'The key language of our age is ethnic nationalism.' Thirty years ago I used to wish that Northern Ireland would get more like the rest of the world: today I fear that the rest of the world is getting more like Northern Ireland. Multi-culturalism may seem undesirable because, first, to dilute the ethnic essence is to sacrifice an electoral asset. The SDLP and the Ulster Unionists are being squeezed by ethnically sterner parties, Sinn Féin and the DUP. And if Sinn Féin aspires to be the custodian of Irish nationalism, at the expense of Fianna Fáil as well as the SDLP, it cannot afford to compromise on core values. Second, ideas like 'multi-culturalism' or 'diversity' are not self-evident goods. They are open to political and conceptual challenge. From one angle, they imply a 'liberal' ethic which can be seen by nationalists as not only state-funded but state-boosting (and hence unionist), and by unionists as promoting a greening of Northern Ireland that weakens the constitutional status quo. (As I write, an Irish-language school in Dunloy, Co. Antrim, has suffered an arson attack.) From another angle, as Michael Morgan recently argued, the 'cultural diversity model [can] place every sort of cultural practice within the same value-free "inclusive" framework: all must be equally respected and tolerated and publicly funded'. Thus, 'Cultural diversity can be twisted to mean that there is no difference, culturally speaking, between such masterpieces of Gaelic culture as The Book of Kells and The Cloughfern Young Conquerors Flute Band.'

Finally, both unionism and nationalism want multi-culturalism on their own terms. In *Being Irish* David Trimble opts for the multi-cultural minimum: 'When discussing identity on the island of Ireland I believe it is dangerous and inappropriate to attempt to integrate existing diversity. One should not try to blend together traditions that are essentially different . . . Instead, our objective should be to find a way in which diverse traditions can be affirmed and enjoyed.' Meanwhile Martin McGuinness speaks of the need to persuade 'our people' of the unionist tradition 'that they are an integral and cherished part of the Irish nation', who 'will not have to give up anything they cherish in what will be a multicultural, multiracial, multilingual secular society'. Familiar political contours lurk beneath the culture-talk of both politicians. The magnetic convergence of culture and politics is the most profound obstacle to multi-culturalism in Northern Ireland. Firstly, it reduces cultural debate to arguments about Orangeism or the Irish language or the ownership of St Patrick. Secondly, it constrains the role of culture in political change. Political ideologies everywhere invoke culture selectively. This applies to the very concept: 'culture' is what must divide Ireland for Trimble, integrate it for McGuinness. Each would take exactly the opposite tack if the UK were in question. And political ideologies choose from culture only those elements that seem to validate their cause. Masses of cultural expression — alternative realities, virtually alternative countries — were ignored while the Free State/Republic fetishised 'Irishness', Northern Ireland its ties with Britain. A new politics for the North would emphasise neglected cultural phenomena, neglected commonalities. If that, too, would be a selective process, it would also be a nice change.

Perhaps 'inter-cultural' is a better term than the somewhat ambiguous 'multi-cultural' for the project of engaging with genuine differences and making them fruitful. In the US, for instance, 'multi-culturalism' signifies the divisive tendency whereby different ethnic groups like to picture themselves as autonomous, and reject the notion of a wider or dominant culture. What may (up to a point) be salutary for post melting-pot America, may not be so for already-ethnic Ireland — where new-style ethnicity (the late twentieth-century stress on 'identity') arrived before old-style ethnicity had departed. Of course, the inter-cultural project confronts practical as well as theoretical obstacles. Our consociational Agreement fits how most people now effectively live in Northern Ireland. The population-shifts caused by the Troubles, whether involuntary or voluntary, mean fewer mixed areas; greater social apartheid; unreasonable demands for local self-sufficiency. (In some people's heads Northern Ireland is a vast prairie which might be infinitely devolved so that nobody ever has to encounter anything that might disturb their cultural complacency.) And, of course, territories are still carved up between paramilitary organisations and controlled by a sinister discipline. Researchers find that 'keeping to your own' seems not only prudent but increasingly desirable and inevitable. Catholic and Protestant Derry are physically divided by the Foyle — the nationalist rhetoric of new Derry's inclusiveness should be taken with a pinch of salt. Working-class areas in Belfast, like small rural towns, continue to consolidate whatever majority they started with. Middle-class Prod-flight from south Belfast to north Down has created new kinds of exclusive community. In her 1993 book *In Search of a State: The Catholics of Northern Ireland* Fionnuala O'Connor writes about a disappointed inter-culturalist middle-class Catholic:

> As he described how he saw the drift in his area repeated in other parts of the North, this man became increasingly depressed. He

seemed equally downcast by attitudes he saw on both sides: the Protestant rush to leave, and among Catholics a lack of enthusiasm for mixing . . . He suspected he knew what lay behind Protestant flight at a personal level: 'They're exporting their kids because the political environment is changing so dramatically . . . But as well as that, I'm nearly afraid to say it — I think they just don't want to live side by side.' On the other hand, he knew that his own yearning for a mixed society was unusual. It was clearly not among the social ambitions of many others: Catholic friends, he said, found it odd that he felt so comfortable with Protestants . . . And what I dislike most: there's a whisper of triumphalism among some of them, that the system is breaking down for the Protestant community, and 'they're beginning to get a taste of their own medicine'.

A few years of peace process will not quickly change settlement patterns or social patterns produced by thirty years of civil war. Even if the Executive survives, everyone talks of 'decades' ahead. And what applies to topography and social intercourse also applies to mental space. A favourite optimistic symbol for an inter-cultural future in Northern Ireland is patchwork. A patchwork artwork, Helen Overley's 'Weave of Diversity', serves as the logo for the Cultural Diversity Group, a body that oversees the cultural role of the Community Relations Council. The image consists of rectangular transparent envelopes, with cultural emblems inside and outside the tubes. The emblems include: Orange and Hibernian banners, a lily, a dove, a red hand, musical instruments, sports equipment, flags, a poppy, Irish dancers, a crucifix, the tokens of feminism and gay sexuality, pigeons, a buddha, a bible, countryside and city. The envelopes overlap in a criss-cross ribbon-like fashion, and the emblems are distinct, but also unexpected, jumbled, fluid. Here is my own patchwork image. Perhaps a realistic map of Northern Ireland as mental space or cultural space would sometimes show black boundary-lines between colours, sometimes unusual shadings where colours run into each other: part Mondrian, part Kandinsky. It was Kandinsky, indeed, who pioneered the notion that the 'either-or' mentality should be replaced by 'both-and'. A Kandinsky flow, with a few propagandist exceptions, fits the map that one might read from the collective work of Northern Irish writers and artists. The creators exploit all the inter-cultural opportunities. They do not ignore the black lines but expose them to the unusual shadings. A recent example was when seven local dramatists took over the derelict Crumlin Road courthouse and jail with their liberating inventions.

A Short History of the Irish Culture War

In time as well as space the cultural question extends beyond 'Northern Ireland'. This component of the UK came bloodily into being because, after Catholic Emancipation in 1829, Irish Protestants perceived themselves to be fighting a rearguard action. Nationalists fail to realise that Ulster unionists do not overlook the all-Ireland context, however they might misrepresent it, but are negatively obsessed by 'Dublin'. Similarly, the all-Ireland context is what gives Ulster nationalists the passive-aggressive faith that their day will come. The 'double minority' paradigm — Protestants in Ireland/Catholics in Northern

Ireland — does most to explain the 'mutual fear-threat relationship' (Faith and Politics Group); the alternations of cultural defence and cultural attack, of insecurity and triumphalism, on both sides. For over 150 years, with remissions, retreats and regroupings, Ireland has been the scene of a *Kulturkampf*: that is, a culture war, in which the two sides have been chiefly defined by religious denomination. Where there has been culture war, we need a cultural peace, a cultural process. Indeed, Ireland's great creative moments, such as the Literary Revival, have either stemmed from inter-cultural endeavour or from resistance to Irish mono-culturalism. As W.B. Yeats put it, with reference to the productive truce that began in the 1890s: 'Before 1891, Unionists and Nationalists were too busy keeping one or two simple beliefs at their fullest intensity for any complexity of thought or emotion.'

In 1989 Roy Foster spoke of how 'round 1900 an inclusive, energetic cultural debate was opening up between brokers of different cultural traditions in Ireland'. Warning against fatalism now, he argued that inter-cultural momentum then could have had a positive outcome. As it turned out, however, Ireland froze into the two would-be mono-cultural entities whose spiritual stagnation is so depressingly evoked by Hubert Butler. Much guilt for that stagnation must be borne by the Churches which did little to alleviate a polarisation that secured their power. I am aware that my stress on religion in this essay may offend nationalists who are unwilling to understand their political consciousness in confessional terms. Protestant politics, in contrast, see-saw between secular (UUP) and religious (DUP) inflections. Yet two authoritative books on Ulster Catholics, O'Connor's *In Search of a State* and Marianne Elliott's *The Catholics of Ulster*, maintain that

Catholicism has been as central as Protestantism to communal (ethnic) self-definition. As Elliott sees it, Catholicism has become invisible 'because it was so successfully subsumed into political culture over three hundred years ago'. She writes of a more recent era:

> In addition to the great processions for the feast of Corpus Christi and the thousands who would turn out for the various confraternities, investitures or funerals of bishops were like alternative state occasions. The Congress of the Catholic Truth Society of Ireland held in Belfast in 1934 attracted 120,000 to its pontifical mass . . . But it was the activities surrounding the 1932 Eucharistic Congress which provided the most stunning example of triumphal pageantry and Catholic devotionalism as a leisure activity. An estimated 100,000 Catholics travelled south for the Phoenix Park Ceremony, and a special high mass was said in Corrigan Park in Belfast for another 80,000 . . . Open-air shrines and arches appeared all over Catholic Belfast . . . It was, proclaimed the *Irish News* in bold headlines, the 'Triumph of Catholic Ireland', and so it was treated by gangs of loyalists who stoned the trains as they departed.

Another study by David G. Holmes has noted the gap between the importance that contemporaries attached to the Eucharistic Congress and its current neglect by historians:

> The discourse surrounding the congress supported a story of Ireland that included past, present and future, but excluded as protagonists those who were not Catholic . . . An Irish identity

had evolved well before the congress, but the particular version of Irish identity that we associate with the Ireland of de Valera . . . was both strengthened and reformed by this event. It was the Eucharistic Congress that cemented the link between Irishness and Roman Catholicism that historians and others associate with Ireland in the period from the 1930s through to the 1960s.

From a Catholic viewpoint, 'bigoted' equals 'Protestant'. One need look no further than Orangeism or Paisleyism or the record of discrimination against Northern Irish Catholics to understand why this is so. Yet, from a Protestant viewpoint, the Catholic Church can seem *institutionally* bigoted in its self-belief as the one true Church — a belief that transfers to the one true Ireland. The recent *Dominus Iesus* statement from the Vatican dismayed Catholic and Protestant ecumenists alike. By the same token, it cheered a Presbyterian minister and leading orangeman, Warren Porter, who praised the 'consistency' and 'honesty' of Rome in keeping the theological boundary-lines clear. If we move from theology to sociology, mixed marriages are equally suspect in both Northern communities. Loyalists, of course, have murderously targeted people in mixed relationships, but Catholic opposition is also expressed in less violent ways. And Fionnuala O'Connor writes: 'Many Catholics in mixed marriages list relatives who have broken off contact, ignored the birth of children, or asked directly if they will now be "betraying your politics like you've betrayed your religion".' That the 'mixed' can seem so problematic, threatening and treacherous is a mark of culture war.

Segregated education has not helped matters, nor was it intended to. In *The Politics of Irish Education 1920-1965*, Sean Farren — the SDLP politician now responsible for higher education in the Executive — concludes:

> The direct Church influence and control over the schools attended by the majority of Irish pupils at primary and secondary level was probably unparalleled elsewhere in the western world . . . The final point to be made about church control and influence is the extent to which it served to sustain and reinforce divisions and antagonisms between Christians in both parts of the country, but especially in the North where religion overlapped so much with politics . . . before education could contribute in a positive manner [to political resolution after 1969], darker forces were at work overshadowing more hopeful developments and reaping the harvest which some of the educational seeds sown in Ireland over these 45 years had helped to produce.

During the last twenty years curricula have been gradually trans-formed North and South. There are many cross-community, cross-border school encounters. There is a small but growing integrated sector. In the Republic, Catholics have entered formerly all-Protestant schools. Some now attend Protestant grammar schools in the North too. Nevertheless, the North's norm of segregation, reinforced by segregated housing, means that cross-community educational exchange, even if it were enthusiastically pursued by every single school (and schools have other things to do) can only be remedial. 'Keeping to your own' is a well-established habit by the time young people leave school. Meetings in the work-force, in city-centre youth culture, at university, may overcome this habit, but not easily. That the Catholic school system became the community's crucial identity-bearer makes it difficult to envisage an integrated state education system for Northern Ireland (this was actually proposed by Stormont in 1923, but opposed by all the Churches). Yet perhaps integrated thinking ought, at least, to begin. In fact, the 'Catholic schools question' epitomises the tension between multi-culturalism, which safeguards identity, and inter-culturalism, which conceives identity as fluid.

The Republic allows more space for fluidity. Yet that did not stop *Irish Times* columnist Eddie Holt claiming in November 2000 that members of the Republic's Catholic middle class had espoused a 'cultural Protestantism' (including Protestant schools) mainly for economic and upwardly-mobile social reasons. In other words, 'mixing' (Holt refers to a 'post-religious' 'pick 'n' mix') is once again suspect: it can have no intellectual or credal content, being a typical Dublin-centred, self-centred betrayal of 'smaller communities' in rural Ireland where 'traditional ties and loyalties naturally remain more robust'. Holt's 'naturally' begs many educational questions. I mention his article to indicate both that the Republic is not yet an exhausted site of cultural battles long ago, and that attitudes there remain crucial to inter-cultural prospects in Northern Ireland. In another recent *Irish Times* article Gordon Linney, the Church of Ireland Archdeacon of Dublin, argued that the Republic's governing class had fallen away from 'the initiative in self-examination and self-criticism' represented by the 1994 Forum for Peace and Reconciliation. Linney writes:

> as a member of a minority most of whose members live in the North, I feel a growing unease at the apparent drift of elements in the political establishment in the South towards a nation-alist/republican alliance with a dated political agenda which by its very nature excludes modern unionism. It seems at times there is a political equivalent to *Dominus Iesus*. We are being inexorably reversed into a pre-Forum past and alienating many in the process, including the entire moderate unionist community.

Linney has in mind issues like decommissioning, policing, retro-spective whitewashing of a republican terror campaign that killed 2,139 people and maimed many more. Of course, bringing Sinn Féin in from the cold has always run the risk of bringing some of the cold in with Sinn Féin. Yet here Irish nationalism may have been productively ambiguous; whereas 'respectable' unionism's treatment of the loyalist ex-paramilitaries can be unproductively hypocritical: a refusal to admit the whole community's implication in appalling violence. It has often been said that if 'the people of Northern Ireland' really 'longed for peace' they would vote differently. Nonetheless, the political rapprochement between all shades of Irish nationalism has changed the previous situation whereby the Republic's alienation from the IRA had made it more receptive to unionism, more wary of northern nation-alism. Such a change, of course, was one objective of the Hume-Adams pact. Ideally, better relations with Ulster Catholics — itself an intercultural move which might lead to exploration of regional differences as well as of repressed political tensions — need not be at the expense of good relations with Ulster Protestants. But the way in which northern nationalism obstructs the latter, and continues to disturb some southern Protestants, suggests that the wider Irish culture war is not over yet. Linney ends by citing Hubert Butler: 'The . . . posthumous apology has no value unless the political narrowness and bigotry that excluded him have gone for ever and are no longer operative.'

North-South/East-West

Even if Ulster Protestants do not succumb to paranoia about 'pan-nationalism', they may become irritated by a new cultural nationalism which internal developments in the Republic have thrown up, and which has propagandist effects. This is a soft-focus 'Irishness' not so much hostile as indifferent to the Protestant or unionist North: an Irishness which has swapped excessive introversion for excessive extroversion. For instance, it regards artworks by Irish people mainly as assets to the national brand-image. In a sense, the spiritual capital of the Celtic Twilight is now being invested by the Celtic Tiger. There may be a suggestion here of getting over (though also betraying) an old inferiority complex regarding Britain and Protestants. The Irish culture war is not only about symbols but about status-symbols. External audiences are important to what has been termed 'Green boosterism': a rhetoric both of the diaspora (Mary Robinson should never have lit that candle) and of an admiring international community. Paddy Logue perfectly epitomises all the above when he writes in the Introduction to *Being Irish*:

> The end to introspection, the turning outwards to the world and
> the new self-confidence which are the results of both the Celtic
> Tiger experience and the involvement in Europe have had other
> remarkable effects. Our cultural influence extends through the
> world in many different forms. This process has been called the
> hibernicisation of Europe but it is fair now to talk of the hiber-
> nicisation of the world. Our music, dance, films, pubs, literature,
> theatre, athletes are everywhere.

Of course, sensible people in the Republic hate this stuff too. Yet
'turning outwards to the world' may correlate with the political
avoidance of problems at home. Just as the Celtic Tiger has exposed
neglect of the Republic's physical (and perhaps civic) infrastructure, so
the Good Friday Agreement has exposed neglect of its conceptual
infrastructure. In a new collection of essays on how the Republic has
been represented — *Writing in the Irish Republic: Literature, Culture,
Politics* — Tony Canavan and Tom Garvin take different lines on
historical 'revisionism'. First, Canavan pronounces its death or failure:
'In cultural terms it was the anti-revisionists who struck the popular
chord. Within the academy, the 1990s saw the revisionist hegemony
challenged.' To perceive the current complexity of Irish historiography
merely as denoting swings of the ideological pendulum, or as an object
for popular vote, seems frivolous. It illustrates, to quote Hubert Butler,
the 'gentle, persistent pressure towards some simple alignment of
Good and Evil, Friend and Enemy'. The polarising impulse in Irish life

seeks to eradicate the opposition instead of continuing the argument. In fact, I doubt whether there can be any real reversal of the significant if insufficient changes that have occurred in the Republic's historical self-understanding, despite claims that the old days were not really so bad (usually from pundits too young to have been there) or the propaganda surrounding commemorations of the Famine and 1798. Thus Garvin discerns an applied revisionism at work:

> A secular patriotism, which does not lean on tribal or religious identities, has evolved in Ireland in recent decades. This relative secularism has made rapprochement between North and South, Britain and Ireland, not only feasible but inevitable and obvious. The process is by no means complete, but it seems that the Irish, a politically rather able people, are well up to completing it in their own good time. Some would see these changes as decadent; others see it as a long-overdue return to normal.

The argument about Irish history is not merely an academic or a southern Irish issue. Nor are so-called 'revisionists' 'taking the pain out of Irish history'. Rather, it has become less possible for anyone to ignore the totality of pain. In *Rethinking Irish History*, Patrick O'Mahony and Gerard Delanty note that, 'Irish historical revisionism is more than an intellectual movement. It is associated with those in the Republic who wish to see a new nation code that would reflect better what they see as the real unfolding of Irish history.' So 'revisionism' is about the conceptual infrastructure — about the Good

Friday Agreement, indeed, as Garvin implies. Further, the more widely a sense of historical complexity is disseminated, the less clear-cut the cultural battle-lines become. Some republicans and loyalists actually acquired respect for each others' narratives in the Maze prison. If Ulster Protestants and Catholics lose even one per cent of their historical-theological certitude it promotes an inter-cultural Northern Ireland. Collective work on regional history, even intensely localised history, has been perhaps the most successful 'cultural diversity' activity in the North.

Northern cultural nationalism, as the West Belfast Festival indicates, is a tougher proposition than vapid boasts of global hibernicisation. But it can live with, and off, Green boosterism, especially in the USA. Meanwhile, to turn to the East-West context of Northern Ireland's cultural condition, the changing UK is less congenial to unionists than the Republic is now to Northern nationalists. Unionists, so to speak, experience revisionism every day — and show the strain. Once upon a time Irish unionism was in tune with the grand narrative of British history. But Ulster Protestants retained past its sell-by date the cultural ideology that cemented the UK during the eighteenth and nineteenth centuries: that 'Britishness' of Protestantism, industry and empire which Linda Colley puts in its most positive light when she writes that Protestantism 'meant much more in this society than just bombast, intolerance and chauvinism. It gave the majority of men and women a sense of their place in history and a sense of worth . . . It gave them identity.' But no longer. Of course, other UK communities have also undergone de-industrialisation, demoralisation and loss of cultural identity bound up with the old Britishness. But history has made Ulster

Protestants more vulnerable. Besides losing former identifications and self-images, they are conscious of a renewed push to secure what can objectively be seen as a historical retreat of Irish Protestantism to the north-east coast and across the sea.

At the 2000 Merriman Summer School, M. Wynn Thomas said of Wales under Margaret Thatcher:

> Her jingoistic Englishness made even the most deferential Welsh feel excluded from her belligerently anglocentric version of Britishness; her blithe denial of the concept of society reawakened Welsh collectivist sentiment; her attack on the miners produced a previously unimaginable common front between Plaid Cymru and the Labour Party; her savage deindustrialisation policy meant that anglicised industrial South Wales felt victimised and superannuated just like Welsh-language culture; the new yuppie class that appeared under her patronage along the urbanised coast of South Wales gave Britishness a bad name among the once proudly hyphenated Welsh-British valleys proletariat.

In Scotland too Thatcherism weakened the union and advanced devolution. And we might note that Welsh nationalism, once exclusively ethnic and language-based, began to take its cue from Scotland's much older 'civic idea of nationhood' (Thomas). This enabled devolutionary co-operation with ex-industrial Labour Wales and moved Welsh nationalism leftwards. In Scotland there has been similar convergence between the Labour Party and the Scottish

National Party on the point of working for Scotland, though not on the national question. Scottish cultural nationalism is more eclectic than the Welsh or Irish variety, and the Labour Party as much as the SNP now emphasises Scottish cultural achievements. All this reflects the degree of autonomy that Scottish institutions have always possessed under the union. Scottish nationalism may occasionally reach for Scotland's Gaelic-Jacobite strand as a Romantic, anti-unionist point of reference. But 'Scots' (the Scots dialect) is just as significant, and none of Scotland's languages — or religions — belongs to any political party. Formerly, the west-coast Catholics who emigrated from Ireland clung to the Labour Party, whereas the SNP was mainly a Protestant formation. Both parties realise, however, that sectarianism is not entirely dead in Scotland.

What are the implications for Ulster Protestants/unionists in their vulnerable situation? First, it is clearly in their interests to emerge from melancholy introversion and take note of how devolution is working elsewhere. Indeed, the Ulster Unionist Assembly member Esmond Birnie has said of the British-Irish Council: 'The BIC is in part visionary. It recognises the strength of human and cultural connections in these islands.' This may revisit the old 'British ties' rhetoric, but it also acknowledges a changed landscape. Second, as David Trimble and his allies seem to have accepted, a 'civic idea', 'civil society', is the name of the devolutionary game. But whereas in Scotland and Wales civic/civil ideals match the historical culture of the main 'union' party (the Labour Party), unionism in Northern Ireland has always been ethnic — despite rhetoric to the contrary — let alone being ready to embrace the local brand of 'Celtic' nationalism.

Thus the conflict between anti- and pro-Agreement unionists is between unionism as a form of ethnic (Ulster/British) nationalism and as a belated 'civic' understanding of Britishness. (Up to a point, a similar conflict exists between Sinn Féin and the SDLP: one that turns on whether the war was fundamentally 'about' the Irish nation or civil rights.) A third lesson for unionists is that not only nationals in devolved Scotland and Wales now value indigenous culture. Traditionally, unionists have been so terrified of indigenous Ulster culture turning out to be 'Irish' in some politically incorrect way, that they developed a vocabulary of transcendental Britishness or Ukanianism. To onlookers, this merely betrayed their provincial cultural cringe. That game too has moved on, since the metropolitan centre no longer plays it in the old way. Finally, unionists should begin to see East-West not simply as 'their' bit of the Agreement; just as Northern nationalists should not hog North-South for themselves.

Regarding the last point: on the one hand, there is a prudential argument. In times of peril unionism reaches for the Scottish roots of the largest Protestant denomination (Presbyterianism), and dwells on the virtues of the 'Ulster Scot' as opposed to the Gael or Anglo-Irishman. This compliment, however, is not always returned by a Scotland wary of political contamination. Thus devolved Scotland displays more enthusiasm for getting together with the Republic than with the North. To mark the opening of the Aberdeen Institute of Irish and Scottish Studies in November 1999, there was a substantial supplement in *The Irish Times*. Introducing it, Paul Gillespie wrote: 'Scotland and Ireland are converging and getting to know one another again.' Not before time, one would think, given the massive historical traffic between the two, although its predominantly northern route partly accounts for the southern Irish perception that Scotland dropped off the map in 1922. But on both sides one senses an underlying desire that Ireland and Scotland should meet as post-Ukanian entities rather than as mutually complicating cultural zones. Thus Bertie Ahern speaks of 'our close Celtic neighbour Scotland', and the Ulster presbyterian minister John Dunlop sounds a cautionary note which unionists and others should heed: 'It is important that the Belfast/Edinburgh axis is strong and is not subsumed into London or Dublin.' Indeed, such an axis could be a corrective to incorrigibly 'Anglo-Irish' (and perhaps Anglican-Catholic) ways of conceiving these islands.

On the other hand, there are cultural reasons why both communities in Northern Ireland should assimilate the complications of Scotland where ethnic markers like language and religion are concerned. Introducing *Gaelic Identities*, Gordon McCoy and Maolcholaim Scott begin:

> The Scottish Gaelic scene is both strange and familiar to Irish speakers. Gaelic movements on both sides of the Irish Sea have much in common: the language classes and learners' culture, struggles for increased status, and the contrast between urban and rural Gaelic speakers. Yet so much in Scotland is unfamiliar to Irish speakers: Gaelic choirs as a focus for learners' activities; ceilidhs held in British Legion halls; the lack of overt nationalism in the revival movement; and what appears most unusual — Free Presbyterians who worship in Gaelic.

To develop Northern Ireland as a truly inter-cultural civic space entails maximising the East-West and North-South connections of all parties. If I have mainly looked at these connections through Protestant/unionist lenses, it is partly owing to the context of this essay, partly because the unionist sense of vulnerability threatens everyone's security. David Porter, a member of ECONI (Evangelical Contribution On Northern Ireland) writes in the autumn 2000 issue of the ECONI journal *Lion & Lamb*:

> Unionism is caught between the civic vision of inclusiveness regardless of religion and culture and the religious exclusion of a militant Protestantism . . . the inheritors of [the evangelical] tradition today are characterised by three traits that dispose them against the politics of accommodation that is on offer and towards a politics of fear; *fundamentalist* in belief and mindset; separatist, with an emphasis on maintaining distinctiveness and distance from those who differ; *apocalyptic*, with a worldview based on an expectation of the world becoming a more hostile place in which to live, at the heart of which is the threat of Catholic domination.

I want to make two points in relation to the foreboding of apocalypse — the destructive and self-destructive political mode personified by Ian Paisley. Firstly, it can be read as a cry of distress in the face of a propaganda war which Ulster Protestants have comprehensively lost. Thus the DUP politician Gregory Campbell speaks of 'a people so vilified and so misrepresented that they must seek a refuge that will not betray them'. Here religious and political fundamentalism fuse in a way that despairs of earthly salvation. But Protestants of whatever political inclination often feel invisible if not doomed. John Dunlop has written of the media blind spot regarding the largest Protestant Church in Northern Ireland: 'Many people in the Presbyterian Church . . . feel like invisible people. It is as if they do not exist . . . It is a humiliating experience for people to be overlooked, misinterpreted or rendered voiceless.' To which Ulster Catholics might well reply: 'So where were you all these years?' Nonetheless, incipient Catholic triumphalism, however understandable, contributes to what I term Depressed Prod Syndrome — DPS. This can even afflict impeccably liberal or quite nationalist Protestants. I have heard one such refer to 'ethnic roll-over time'. Thus the Protestant community now tends to see itself as the victim. Ludicrously, Drumcree has become an attempt to claim the victim position — obviously Protestants are not yet very good at it. More generally, if Catholics are reluctant to relinquish victimhood (what Elliott calls their 'sense of occupying the moral heights against the victimiser') and Protestants seek to claim it, this hardly provides a basis for equal inter-cultural encounters. John Dunlop's book is called *A Precarious Belonging*. Susan McKay entitled her recent study *Northern Protestants: An Unsettled People*. The cover alone might bring on DPS. It features a union jack and an Ulster flag tied to a withered branch stuck in an apocalyptic wasteland at Drumcree.

Secondly, the apocalyptic strain in Protestant consciousness is partly a function of the Irish culture war. One way in which any ethnic group seeks to unsettle another is by claiming that they have an inferior culture or none at all. Unionists used to scoff at the Irish language and traditional music (regardless of Protestant participation in both) as primitive. More recently, 'culture' has been seen in some quarters as a Catholic thing just as bigotry is a Protestant thing. It is now commoner to find charges that Ulster Protestants 'have no culture' or that Orangeism is the sum of Protestant culture (as contrasted with all-singing, all riverdancing Catholics). The history of the arts and sciences in the North refutes both these politicised stereotypes. Northern Irish people involve themselves in a range of Britannic and European traditions (including theological traditions) which are not crudely stamped Orange or Green. Nonetheless, as in Scotland, fundamentalists have traditionally placed taboos on certain kinds of artistic expression. And there are reasons, to do with different community structures, why working-class Protestants might internalise the charge of being cultureless. McKay reports the Progressive Unionist Party leader David Ervine as follows: 'He said that after the agreement there would be a greater appreciation of culture. "Nationalist areas have cultural centres, heritage centres, they have worked feverishly for their culture. Now you look at the Field at Edenderry. There isn't even a toilet."' A project has just been announced which will address 'the cultural and community deficit' in working-class Protestant areas. Its spokesman said that when a group of Protestants were asked to describe the roots of their identity 'they came up with a bag of dolly-mixtures'. It surprised political observers when the Ulster Unionist Party chose Culture, Arts and Leisure as one of its ministries (Sinn Féin had expected to bag it). Apparently this was no accident, but rather a recognition that culture counts. The minister, Michael McGimpsey, has so far seemed equally attentive to North-South, East-West, and the contested regional space between.

Cultural War and Peace

Some people see the peace process as war by other means. It might alternatively be seen as a pressing-back of conflict to the cultural field or as a new phase of the Irish culture war. The parades issue, to some extent deliberately fomented by Sinn Féin, is a case in point. And sometimes cultural difference comes down to the difference between being beaten with baseball bats or with hurleys. Much depends on whether the Agreement parties really desire an inter-cultural sharing of Northern Ireland or whether, now that culture has become more significant, they will build up their own constituency by intensifying the politicisation of culture. The latter trend is probably inevitable: the important thing is that 'civil society' should be strong enough to complement or counter it. An Alliance Party politician has posed the troubling question: 'Do we have peace at the cost of reconciliation?'

In fact, brooding on culture has been a favourite occupation of civil society for over a decade. The Cultural Traditions Group (now Cultural Diversity Group) was established in 1988. Through the Community Relations Council, the CDG has supported conferences, exhibitions, books, cultural activities by local communities, every kind of historical and linguistic enquiry, and the exploration of symbols. More broadly, it has created a philosophy and language which have influenced politics (at district council level too). This influence can be ambiguous, as when David Trimble uses diversity-speak to stress separateness, or when (as Michael Morgan complains) value-free relativeness seems to legitimise dubious practices as 'culture'. But to support research on Orangeism, or to assist the preservation of archives and insignia, is not necessarily to endorse the Order's political behaviour. It may, indeed, promote reflection on that behaviour. The motto of the original Cultural Traditions Group was 'expression-education-exploration-exchange-debate'. Critique, if not always achieved, was intended to qualify affirmation. The next stage of cultural diversity work will be influenced by its new location in the Department of Culture, Arts and Leisure. Fresh factors are the potentially structural role of 'diversity thinking' in government and the way in which 'multi-culturalism' has suddenly moved up the British (the Parekh Report) and European agendas. For once, Northern Ireland may be ahead of the pack. Thus North-South liaison might prompt the Republic to cultural-diversity work on its conceptual infrastructure. And perhaps we could sometimes talk about South-North as denoting like East-West an axis of discovery. The conference reports of Encounter, established in 1983 by the British and Irish governments to promote mutual contact, also provide highly relevant blueprints.

I want to glance at three cultural areas — religion, commemoration and language — to illustrate the conflict between the old dispensation in the North and the (one hopes) emergent order struggling to be born. These three areas are the core areas of European ethnic self-definition. Religion returns us to the origins of the Irish culture war, though in a curiously sidelined way. For instance, it has been left out of the 'cultural diversity' loop or may have been too fly to get caught. A 1997 survey of *Attitudinal Variations among Churchgoers in Belfast* concludes that, 'Religion matters in Belfast and the religious spaces that dot the urban landscape are of immense significance even though they remain *terrae incognitae* to the eye of much scholarship and political commentary.' It is another unremarked and remarkable fact that the churches can still perceive themselves as part of the solution rather than as central to the problem (Colm Tóibín has said that they should be down on their knees apologising). Johnston McMaster challenges this perception in his Catalyst pamphlet *Churches on the Edge: Responding Creatively to a Changing Time*. He asks whether the churches can change or must become 'exiled in a past which will no longer have meaning':

> The churches cannot preach repentance without living repentance. This will involve honestly acknowledging roles and responsibilities in the past which have contributed towards community division, conflict and violence. Doctrinal formulations and ways of making truth claims have had divisive and even tragic consequences . . . Much of what has been practised has been civil religion, where God has been nationalised and used to give legitimacy to political arrangements of power or aspirations which are dominating and excluding. The cross has been the banner of an army or a weapon of conflict over against the other.

Despite the committed work of Corrymeela, Glencree, the Irish School of Ecumenics and the Irish Council of Churches, despite co-operation between church leaders during the Troubles, despite the 1993 publication of *Sectarianism: A Discussion Document*, ecumenical and anti-sectarian action has proceeded very slowly on the ground. Duncan Morrow, reviewing attitudes in bitterly segregated Armagh after the events at Drumcree in 1996, comments: 'No Church in Northern Ireland gives any guidance or has any policy of support or organisation for clergy about how to deal with sectarianism in a practical form.' He attributes this to the potentially 'explosive impact on the internal structures of the churches'.

Yet there are instances of profound interchange, such as that between Clonard Monastery and Fitzroy Presbyterian Church, while Catholic and Protestant clergy preaching in one another's pulpits has become quite normal (although not, of course, in the fundamentalist sector). Local Inter-Church Forums, which include clergy and laity, have been set up. These allow for continued dialogue and a common response to local events. This system tragically proved itself in Omagh where the local Forum served as a crucial mechanism both after the bomb and in relation to the movingly inclusive commemoration a year later. The Church of Ireland has appointed a 'peace agent' in every congregation. The Presbyterians show a mixed picture in that they have become politically more liberal but theologically more rigid. However, an important finding of the Belfast survey was of 'significant variation within each of the two sets of churchgoers — Catholics and Protestants — as regards religious belief and practice, public and private morality, cross-community relations and experience, and [political] motivations'. The Troubles forced people into pan-Protestant and pan-Catholic loyalties which might crack in interesting ways, both religious and political, if the premium on cohesion were to weaken. Protestant views have already fissured as regards Drumcree and the Orange Order. This should be seen as potentially a mark of self-critical strength rather than as a blow to unity. It is relevant that the Catholic laity in the Republic engages more critically with the Church than does the laity in the North.

ECONI and Catalyst (based in the Church of Ireland) are examples of internal critique. Their publications draw on people of other religious affiliations, but these groups are motivated by what they see as the historical inadequacies of evangelicalism and the Church of Ireland respectively: inadequacies, that is, as regards the relationship between faith and politics. It is significant that neither group takes a secular view but looks for a deeper Christianity uncontaminated by the urge to fly union jacks from steeples. ECONI, which has made a practical contribution to the peace process, seeks to identify and apply 'biblical principles pertinent to a Christian response to the Northern Ireland conflict', and also to bring issues raised by that conflict back to the bible. It asks questions like whether 'God and Ulster' should be separated and how you might affirm faith by 'border crossings'. The first pamphlet in its Pathways series 'describes some of the approaches to evangelical-Roman Catholic relationships advocated by mainstream evangelicals in Northern Ireland'. Catalyst began its activities with a set of lectures (by such figures as Enda McDonagh, John Dunlop and Geraldine Smyth) that examine the contradiction between 'civil religion' and 'Forgiveness, Healing and Peace'. There followed pamphlets criticising the Church of Ireland's stance on integrated education, its fudges with respect to Drumcree and church flags (where the General Synod's wishes have not been implemented), its connivance at an identification between the Church and unionism, its

failure to tackle sectarianism. In 1999 a Catalyst pamphlet stated bluntly: 'The Drumcree crisis has dealt a profound challenge to the internal order of the Church and more importantly made a mockery of its purported ecumenism and of the "Theological Reflections" underpinning the work of the Committee [on Sectarianism].' All this critique is encouraging, even though it has barely dented Northern Ireland 'civil religions'. We are still a long way (why?) from Geraldine Smyth proposed 'interchurch commission with a strongly inclusive base which would actively address the obstacles to wholeness between the churches themselves, and create opportunities for mutual education theological colleges and at inter-denominational level'.

In Northern Ireland commemoration is an ethnic site where religion, politics and history powerfully fuse. It is not only a matter specific monuments, statues and graves. The whole area operates *lieu de mémoire*: territory marked outwardly by competing symbol inwardly by communal understandings of history. To de monuments or attack commemorative ritual (as at Enniskillen) routine act of culture war. It expresses the desire to erase both cultural presence and cultural memory of the perceived Other desire can be detected on both sides of the parades issue. Comm ration is not just reactive or passive but a reinforcement of m kinship bonds and hence a political agent. To commemorate I Sunday or Internment or the Boyne or the world wars is al contemporary political intervention. At the same time, it prom cult of the dead, the ancestors. Malachi O'Doherty ob 'Catholicism and republicanism offer a form of immortality memory of those who honour the marytrs . . . Republicanism

itself in part for the work of respecting the dead.' In unionism too there can be a vicious circle of self-entrapment whereby commemoration of sacrifice breeds further sacrifice. There is a martyr-cult of Billy Wright as of Bobby Sands. And the addition of peace doves to the reconstituted Enniskillen war memorial was not liked by every local Protestant (the doves were twice vandalised) because it broke the cycle of militaristic blood-bonding.

There has, indeed, been some progress on shared commemoration as a function of shared history. The Ulster Society, for instance, invited a range of people to reflect on the pros and cons of Remembrance Day. The most significant example of commemorative ecumenism is the Peace Park at Messines in Belgium inaugurated by President Mary McAleese and Queen Elizabeth II in November 1998 and dedicated to the participation of Irish people in both world wars. Similarly, the Great War is being rescued from its exclusive invocation by Ulster Protestant memory (particularly of the Somme). Ulster Catholic involvement has been reclaimed by historians and others. Nonetheless, neither side necessarily appreciates such inter-cultural adjustments of cherished historical narratives. The poppy is still seen by most Catholics as a coat-trailing Orange symbol. A recent Remembrance Sunday vox pop on Radio Ulster found ignorance and indifference in west Belfast, enthusiasm in east Belfast.

Commemorating more remote events is inextricable from the question of how Northern Ireland is to 'remember' the last thirty years. Nothing exposes the difficulty of change more than the difficulty of remembrance. In the late 1990s the peace process brough' remembering and forgetting (perhaps prematurely) into the politic

foreground. For example, Jane Leonard examined *Memorials to the Casualties of the Conflict: Northern Ireland 1969 to 1997*. And Sir Kenneth Bloomfield produced *We Will Remember Them: The Report of the Northern Ireland Victims Commissioner*. The latter's brief was to look into the possibility of shared Troubles memorials. Bloomfield concludes that the best options here are practical help for victims/survivors and non-physical memorial schemes that promote education and reflection. An ambitious project of the latter kind is already underway: An Crann/The Tree. Bloomfield also proposes a physical 'Northern Ireland Memorial' 'to be set in a peaceful location among beautifully landscaped gardens' and incorporating local artworks. There are already several public sculptures whose commemorative message is reconciliation. For instance, one was recently unveiled in the grounds of Stormont. It portrays two bowed figures weeping and flowing into each other's arms and hence becoming one body. A press photograph captured an amusing contrast with the body language of the sculpture's dual unveilers: David Trimble and Seamus Mallon, then bitterly at odds over Trimble's suspension of Sinn Féin ministers from North-South meetings. Jane Leonard shows, unsurprisingly, that partisan Troubles memorials greatly outnumber general memorials. Thus she warns against optimism that the latter will soon command popular assent. Nonetheless, the Omagh commemoration will continue to do so. Perhaps the most widely effective general memorial so far has been *Lost Lives: The Stories of the Men, Women and Children who Died as a Result of the Northern Ireland Troubles*, compiled by four Northern Ireland journalists. The poignant complexity of this archive resists the conscription of individual deaths into the ferocious categories which are liable to cause more.

To turn to the language question by way of a digression. It is clearly an excellent thing if working-class Protestants seek to make good 'the cultural and community deficit'. This does redress the traditional Ukanianism/cultural cringe of middle-class unionism (earlier combated by the now-influential 'regionalist' ideas of the poet John Hewitt). It should also restore a kind of self-understanding that many working-class Protestants did indeed possess before the Troubles obliterated their socialist traditions. Yet such initiatives should hopefully not recruit loyalist cultural warriors to fight republican cultural warriors. There is a symptomatic example of this in a more middle-class unionist environment: the successful campaign on behalf of Ulster Scots. A significant context for the campaign was the perceived advantage (including funding) secured by the Irish language movement in the North during the past two decades. Yet that movement itself is internally divided. When republicanism decided (in 1982) that cultural nationalism required the language as its key ethnic marker (thus copying the Gaelic League of 1915) it wrested control away from Belfast's more traditional *gaeilgeóirs* — inclined to be middle-class, constitutional nationalist schoolteachers. The momentum for this derived from the language's function as a form of resistance in the Maze Prison. A third factor was added when the government-sponsored cultural traditions policy led to the setting-up of Ultacht Trust in 1989. The Trust's remit is to fund Irish language projects from whatever source, and hence make it available to Protestants as well as Catholics: a 'common heritage' philosophy to which some unionists indeed subscribe. Both government funding and the decoupling of the Irish language from nationalism — its promotion as culture rather than politics, or as inter-cultural rather than mono-cultural — have been problematic in republican west Belfast.

The campaign for Ulster Scots exhibits some similar features. Viewed as culture it can be seen as a welcome attempt, in keeping with academic interest in the riches of Northern Hiberno-English, to call attention to the Scots linguistic tradition in Ulster: a tradition which influences most people's accents and which has a small but significant literary component. However, the Ulster Scots lobby wants more than this. They want Ulster Scots to be treated as a language and thus given parity with English and Irish. Hence their successful effort to get it recognised as a language by the European Bureau of Lesser-Used Languages. For academic linguists, Ulster Scots, like Scots in general, is a *dialect* not a *language*: this distinction is not a value judgement, but reflects the way in which the relation between Scots and 'English', of which Scots is the northern variety, has evolved historically. But the Ulster Scots lobby has also succeeded in having Scots named as an autonomous language in the Good Friday Agreement:

> All participants recognise the importance of respect, under-standing and tolerance in relation to linguistic diversity; including in Northern Ireland, the Irish language, Ulster Scots and the language of the various ethnic communities, all of which are part of the cultural wealth of the island of Ireland.

As John Kirk has pointed out, for Ulster Scots to operate as a language — into which, for instance, proceedings of the Assembly must be translated — requires massive financial and intellectual resources. In effect, what has been proposed is the *invention* of a language: oral pronunciation is being translated into a rather arbitrary orthography. Extraordinary Ulster Scots neologisms and archaisms are causing some laughter. Also, in Scotland itself Scots has no such status, despite enjoying a significant revival as a cultural and literary resource — the more productive interest it potentially has in Northern Ireland too. (Writers, such as John Hewitt, were interested in Ulster Scots long before the lobby existed.) Kirk comments: 'In Scotland, Scots is currently better off linguistically and poorer off politically. In Northern Ireland it is the opposite.' But perhaps the twin politicisations of language in Northern Ireland illustrate the insularity of the local culture war: as when the Ulster Scots lobby disregards what it can learn from Scotland or when west Belfast sees itself as the epicentre of Irish language revival in this island. Thus East-West and North-South can help us again. It is a good thing that the Irish language, Ulster Scots and English are obliged to meet on the North-South language body: *An Foras Teanga/Tha Boord o Leid*. Perhaps this will eventually prise Ireland's languages out of the symbolic domain where culture war has its being. In the meantime, Aodán Mac Póilin of the Ultach Trust has described the peace process as 'providing the ideal conditions for the politics of outrage, swagger and emblematic posturing', and making 'the language question . . . likely to be the battleground of much of the politico/cultural shadow-boxing of the future'.

Conclusions

If this has been mainly a historical essay, I have no crystal ball. If it has been mainly a pessimistic essay, premature optimism has betrayed us before. If I have dwelt on culture war rather than inter-cultural peace, it is to stress what is at stake, and the political will required all round to make Northern Ireland work as a pluralistic society.

My conclusions are a mix of analysis and prescription. Since the ceasefires (as the cultural politics of religion, commemoration and language indicate) there has been a more conspicuous argument, often within the supposed blocs, between those who 'keep one or two simple beliefs at their fullest intensity' (to quote Yeats) and those who do not. The latter are in the minority, and may be fiercely resisted and resented, like Hubert Butler. The paradox of the Good Friday Agreement is that it was built on the extremes but the centre is the only ground where it can hold. And there are many who think that the Agreement's language does not correspond to the lived complexity of their own identities. Real people's variegated cultural practice, as I have stressed, can make Northern Ireland's narrow cultural ideologies seem lunatic. Or perhaps it is a wider matter, to quote Tom Garvin, of Ireland 'returning to normal' after its twentieth-century excesses.

Nonetheless, disappointed liberals (a tautology in Northern Ireland) should not always bemoan the slowness of distrustful, war-conditioned people to move beyond agreement to settlement. Nobody is free from the polarising reflexes. And if reports, conferences, exhibitions, think-tanks and books were enough, the Northern Ireland question would have been solved long ago — though all the cogitation at least shows that 'simple beliefs' are simply wrong. It also provides a database (local publishers have played a huge part in this) to serve the future. There is, too, what one might call the 'Troubles class': people from every background, not all middle-class quangocrats, who have been involved in cross-community efforts to build civil society. This class has never existed before. Indeed, it now seems as if everyone you meet has some advisory or executive role to keep them off the streets.

If I had a crystal ball, I would ask it to tell me what Northern nationalists want, or whether they know that themselves. Malachi O'Doherty comments: 'Unionists have to declare their limits every day, nationalists never have to declare them at all.' If the Agreement is seen (by both sides) as provisional or transitional, just another arena for symbolic tug-of-war, it will fail. A shared regional locus of allegiance must evolve, whatever other horizons beckon. Most of the ministers in the Executive appear to have a notion of such a locus. And Marianne Elliott is not unrepresentative when she talks of wanting to affirm her 'Northernness', and argues that the two main communities in the North have been more shaped by their proximity than by any other historical agency. She and Susan McKay agreed at a recent public debate that both Protestants and Catholics tend to see the other community as more confident. So parity of security may be more important than parity of esteem, or the unionists will fold their tents and the nationalists never leave theirs. Elliott thinks that the Catholic community is in transition: she is not sure to what. But contexts change people more than people change contexts. Even Sinn Féin may mutate, as it has done, up to a point, on district councils.

In *Eureka Street* Robert McLiam Wilson imagines Belfast as a novel which would integrate all its divided spaces: 'The city's surface is thick with its living citizens. Its earth is sown with its many dead. The city is a repository of narratives, of stories. Present tense, past tense or future. The city is a novel.' Belfast's material infrastructure is developing more rapidly than its civic infrastructure, but they mirror one another's unfinished state: holes and cranes everywhere as in Leipzig or Dresden, high-rising hotels and offices, south Belfast colonised by apartment blocks, the city's lost centre being reinvented by the Waterfront Hall, and the Odyssey (part fun palace, part science park), Celtic Tiger money in town, boutiques replacing home bakeries on the Lisburn Road, paramilitaries with nasty little earners, more film-makers now than poets, the mooted 'writers' square' in the Cathedral Quarter — that touch of Temple Bar — the Belfast City Arts Awards (the City Council's Arts Committee is enthusiastically chaired by Tom Hartley of Sinn Féin), Belfast's aspiration to be European City of Culture.

Meanwhile North-South and East-West are an economic and cultural fact — in trains, cars, planes, in the increasing number of non-local voices around. We will never know what traffic, what enrichment, the lost years prevented. Northern Ireland is potentially a diversified European region where you can live in three places at once (Ireland/Britain/'Ulster') — a liberating condition — not a place that fails to be two other places. The media available here prove this point. The alarming condition of Bosnia affords a timely warning against retreat to mono-cultural polarisation. Bosnia is now divided between its old inter-cultural ethos and nationalist parties that appeal beyond its borders to Serbia and Croatia. Thus, besides parity of security, there should be parity of pressure whereby the 'sovereign governments' impel unionists and nationalists towards one another while yet making them feel loved. The Northern Irish problem, however, challenges very deep assumptions about the UK and the Republic. Some sovereignty, as well as traditional self-understanding, may have to be sacrificed to a more Scandinavian concept of the archipelago: to the indivisible 'weave of diversity', to inter-culturalism in every direction.

Strangers in their Own Country:
Multi-Culturalism in Ireland

DECLAN KIBERD

Introduction

The seductive charm of Irish culture no longer seems to work in quite the old way. A *céad míle fáilte* is not extended to all new arrivals any more. Yet the historical capacity of the Irish to assimilate waves of incomers should never be underestimated. Eight centuries ago, after all, the Normans became 'more Irish than the Irish themselves'. Who is to say that the latest group of arriving Nigerians might not know the same destiny? If there is no zeal like the zeal of the convert, there may be no Irishness quite like that of the recent recruit.

The fear of being assimilated too readily to Irish culture haunted those colonisers who came in the armies of the English queen, Elizabeth I. Their official artists painted portraits of men who had gone native and been barbarised by contact with Gaelic culture. In them, hybridity, far from being a desirable state of cultural fusion, was seen as a negation of humanity itself, as two discrepant codes cancelled one another out, leaving the victim a prey to evil instinct and uncontrolled lasciviousness. On the other side, Gaelic poets lambasted those overlords who were keen to anglicise themselves, dubbing them half-breeds (*'a dhream gaoidhealta gallda'*). Nobody wanted to be a hybrid in those far off, pre-postmodern days: yet somehow quite a lot of writers (and, one assumes, ordinary persons) managed the trick.

By the eighteenth century, macaronic songs and ballads were all the rage in a patently bicultural community, yet the fear on both sides of being wholly absorbed by the other never went away. It surfaced again at the start of the twentieth century in the claim by D. P. Moran that the Gael must be the element which absorbed — a claim which simply underlined the fact that by then it was the Gael who was being co-opted massively by the forces of the English language. When the new Irish state of the 1920s and 1930s appeared intent on defining itself in mainly Catholic and Gaelic terms, Moran's counter-thesis might appear to have staged a late rally: and even today his statement has the power to terrify some critics, who are so fixated on it that they ignore the more progressive elements in his thinking. Routinely, they cite it as further proof of a covert assimilationist tendency in Irish nationalism, whose siren-call to unionists must be resisted. Yet that same siren-call is all but inaudible to Africans and Eastern Europeans. Suddenly, the fear of assimilation seems to have struck the assimilators.

Yet the stubborn facts of history remain. Those English who have 'opted' for Ireland have been effortlessly assumed into the national narrative: from the fictional John Broadbent to the factual Jack Charlton, Ireland has gone on bearing out Bernard Shaw's claim that it is one of the last spots on earth still producing the ideal Englishman of history. In recent years, the number of converts has, if anything, increased. When Daniel Day-Lewis pronounced his win at the Oscars a triumph for Ireland, he effectively dismantled the English-when-they-win, Irish-when-they-lose equation. But he *chose* Irishness, just as much as the Anglo-Normans did before him: in neither case was it forced upon a hapless victim.

There has never been any problem in embracing such figures, despite the fact that in some senses they were products of the traditional 'enemy'. So why the reported reluctance to embrace Nigerians or Romanians? Many people have been shocked by racist attacks on foreigners (not all of them confined to black visitors) and some have wondered whether this is a new phenomenon. Back in the 1970s, when the late Phil Lynott sang 'Whiskey in the Jar', there was little evidence of such intolerance: or even in the 1980s when soccer fans sang the praises of Paul McGrath (although the famous 'ooh-aah' chant had something slightly iffy about it). Perhaps such figures were sufficiently rare as not to seem threatening: what Joyce's Mr Deasy said of the Jews might have been indicated of the blacks — that Ireland had the distinction of never having persecuted them, because it had the sense never to let any numbers of them in. Yet even in those decades, change was afoot. I had a young friend who went to England and when I warned him about the danger of racist attack on the streets of London, he laughed and said: 'Nobody there minds my skin colour: it's only when they hear my Dublin accent that the trouble starts.'

It would be too simple to explain the recent racist outbreaks as a legacy of the colonial system (in which so many Irish served) or even as a copycat version of contemporary yob culture in England. After all, Irish soccer fans have not bothered to emulate the hooliganism of their English counterparts. Nor can it be mainly an after-effect of the encounter between triumphalist Catholic missionaries and African or Asian communities. Many of those Nigerians who have come to Ireland did so in the hope that the people would be as kindly and civilised as those missionaries who taught them at schools and cared for them in medical centres: and they have reported themselves as shocked by the blatant difference in behaviour.

Liberal intellectuals, who had long viewed Irish racism as a largely North American phenomenon, have also been amazed. While Phil Lynott was being acclaimed in Dublin as the inventor of Celtic Rock, over in Boston the lace-curtain Irish who voted for the Kennedys were also quite capable of refusing to share buses and schools with black neighbours. Nor were these problems of recent vintage. Tensions between the two communities went back to the 1840s, when emancipated black Americans lodged formal complaints that the arrival of the Irish was reducing the value of real estate in their neighbourhoods. A century and a half later, a more inflected version of this complaint surfaced with the claim that those scholars who placed Irish Studies in a postcolonial category were really guilty of gazumping black and Hispanic academics in the search for university posts under affirmative action programmes.

Back home in Ireland (and nearby in Britain), relations between Irish and Africans seemed far less tense. Bob Geldof invoked a communal memory of famine in helping to make his own people the largest per capita contributors to Third World relief in Live Aid. In the arts an emerging talent like Roddy Doyle could build an entire comic novel around the contention that the Irish were the blacks of Europe: and *The Commitments* became a film which enjoyed popular success. By 1990 Brian Friel had created in *Dancing at Lughnasa*, a play which explored analogies between Ugandan culture and the harvest festivals of Donegal. Its central character is a returned priest who himself 'went native' in Africa, losing the capacity to distinguish between the codes of the two cultures. Again, though a play by a complex artist might seem to appeal only within the traditional constituency of liberal intellectuals, Friel's masterwork won huge audiences, not just at home but overseas, and most of all among the American Irish.

The backdrop to those debates was, of course, the return of many priests, nuns and 'development' workers from missionary activity. Many brought with them radical new ideas about democratising parish life or applying the principles of liberation theology, learned in Africa or Latin America. Ireland, which had once given a lead to other decolonising peoples, now seemed to be following their example. Nor was this wholly surprising. Missionaries are in the business of transforming consciousness, unlike military governors or colonial administrators, who simply need to know how to give orders and impose rules. Once you make an appeal at the level of the spirit, you are open to a counter-appeal: and that is what happened to many missionaries, like Friel's Father Jack or to the returned theologians of liberation.

Anyone who studies Irish art over the past two decades cannot but be impressed by the amount of inspiration derived from other cultures, mostly in the Third World. What is even more remarkable is that in every case the foreign input, though major, has somehow assisted some element of traditional Irish culture to present itself more stunningly to a modern world audience. At one level, there is the marvellous fusion of Latino elements with native forms in Riverdance (which has obvious parallels with Latino influence in theology); at another, there is the Caribbean collaboration of Seamus

Heaney with his fellow-Nobellist Derek Walcott (with analogies in the fusions of style achieved in various musical bands); and, even at the level of high theory, the inspiration derived by David Lloyd and other critics from the Subaltern Studies Group in India seems to replicate the uses to which W. B. Yeats put Indian culture early in the twentieth century.

In the time of Yeats and Joyce, the Irish had little difficulty in identifying with people of colour. Popular magazines like *Pat* in the 1880s and 1890s were filled with cartoons on the theme, of which Joyce would make much in the 'Cyclops' section of *Ulysses*. There the drinkers in Barney Kiernan's pub make common cause with those African slaves recently defended by Roger Casement. The entire tradition of comparative analysis reached a climax in Richard Ned Lebow's book *White England and Black Ireland,* which suggested that the Paddy and Sambo stereotypes had worked in distressingly similar ways, creating a perceptual prison for the English which left them quite unable to recognise what was actually happening on the ground.

Against that rich background, one might reasonably ask where the roots of Irish racism are to be found. There are some commentators who believe that much of what is being expressed is not racism in the strict sense so much as distress signals emitted by local communities, who find the ecology of their street or village massively disturbed by a bureaucratic central government, which suddenly 'plants' refugees in their midst. The 'Corofin effect' has been replicated in more than one rural town: and the government's failure to brief or persuade communities on the positive potentials of its policy has been at times lamentable. Journalists have managed to convince themselves that all forms of protest against such policies much be racist in tinge: yet most of the trouble spots featured in media reports of 1999 have since settled down, once local people began to come to terms with their new neighbours. If there was some racist element in the initial outcry — and there surely was — it was often broken down once first-hand relationships began. That complex was long ago observed in attitudes to the English, whom the Irish were supposed to dislike 'in theory', but often came to love as individuals. The accusatory tone of some media reports hindered rather than helped progress, for the old journalistic obsession with trouble and strife may sell papers, but often at the cost of increasing the sense of crisis.

In a similar way, it is sometimes hard to fathom whether the jibes and punches thrown at Nigerians in inner-city Dublin's Parnell Street are manifestations of race hatred or of a beleaguered community seeking to defend itself as such. 'We fought the culchies when we had to,' said one veteran of a night's brawl, 'and then we fought the cops. And now we have to fight the darkies.' The elision there suggests an advanced paranoia about outside groupings, but whether it is classical racism is a moot point.

Yet racism of the most ugly kind undeniably exists in Irish society: and the presence of ever-growing numbers of refugees and migrants from overseas has brought it to the surface, making all foreigners (not just people of colour) arguably more vulnerable than once they were. It is probable that in other countries of western Europe anything from 10 per cent to 15 per cent of the community harbours such prejudices against guest-workers: and the same is probably true in Ireland. In order to account for the scale of this phenomenon, it may be useful to return to the fear of hybridity with which I began.

Humans sometimes display a dreadful need to make other people more like them. Irish people may feel this desire more than most. Even our 'liberal' press finds it hard to understand or speak respectfully of those who don't endorse all elements of the liberal agenda. The French are a bit like this too. Wherever they went as colonisers, they felt ratified rather than mocked when natives perfectly imitated them, to the extent of awarding special prizes to Africans who wrote like Frenchmen and Frenchwomen.

Official Irish policy towards asylum-seekers, as spelled out in the 1999 Illegal Immigrants Trafficking Bill, works in a somewhat similar way. Anyone who fails to gain asylum has just fourteen days in which to appeal, despite the fact that ordinary citizens of the Irish Republic have up to six months in which to seek reviews of verdicts. This was one of the clauses which President Mary McAleese found questionable enough to refer to the Supreme Court, which went on to vindicate it. That clause has interesting psychological implications. For instance, the extreme speed with which the appeal is to be processed suggests a problem in the official mind with the 'in-between' state of the applicant. Either the applicant 'becomes Irish' straight away or not at all: and there can be no sustained and troubling period of ambiguity. Either he or she is a wonderful addition to our society or a damned nuisance — but nothing in between.

A further aspect of the judgement is its ready acceptance that the political rights of nationals and non-nationals are not necessarily the same. The ruling of Judge Ronan Keane states:

> The non-national or alien constitutes a discrete category of persons whose entry, presence and expulsion from the State may be the subject of legislative and administrative measures which would not, and in many of its aspects could not, be applied to its citizens. The rights, including fundamental rights, to which non-nationals may be entitled under the Constitution do not always coincide with the rights protected as regards citizens of the State, the right not to be deported being an obvious and relevant example.

In reporting this judgement, Carol Coulter of *The Irish Times* remarked that this went against the spirit of some previous adjudications, which tended to give to non-citizens the same rights as citizens, once they were before the courts of the state, on the principle that the rights of man are universal. The new distinction seemed to reflect a harmonisation of immigrant law across the European Union. Such harmonisation might not be a bad thing in itself, if only to prevent states from deporting immigrants to hard-line regimes for summary despatch: but the effect in this case was to make Ireland as hard-line as everywhere else. Patricia McKenna MEP observed that 'There is something seriously wrong with our Constitution if it cannot afford all people equal rights of access to the courts and surely it is our Constitution that should be amended to reflect modern-day reality.'

The issue broached here is central. Although the sovereignty of nation states has been eroded in recent decades, they are likely to remain with us for many years to come. In the absence of a universal political system, people will have to ask themselves what happens in such a context to stateless persons. It seems that one can as little survive without a nation as without a gender. The need is, therefore, to develop a legal code which offers real protection to foreigners. The problem has been summed up in a savagely satirical question put by Julia Kristeva: 'Is he fully a man if he is not a citizen?' If a foreigner is defined as one who is not a citizen of the country in which she/he resides, then where does that leave her/his political rights (such as the right to vote)? Most foreigners are useful contributors to the national economy and payers of taxes, yet their exclusion from the voting process ultimately denies them influence over decisions which affect their lives. It should be obvious that a process of law-making which excludes them may easily lead to a disinclination to respect state laws, or to respect the entire culture which is bound up with those laws.

The Gardaí have done their best to negotiate the new challenges, and a special unit has been set up to educate members of the force in the specificities of Muslim and other cultures. That wise example should be followed more generally in state schools, which should anyway have long ago offered basic classes in world religions and cultures. What militated against such study in the past was the exceptionalist philosophy of Ireland as a unique island, comparable to nowhere else. The Roman Catholic dogma taught in most schools evoked other –isms only to discount them. Those Irish people who eventually found themselves living next door to Muslims or Rastas had to learn about their codes in less theoretical ways: but now that the home society is becoming so variegated, there is an unanswerable case for such study. Once these classes begin, students may even find that island status provokes a good point of contact with, say, Caribbean peoples, even as the general Catholic background could be a useful aid in understanding Hispanic groups. What were once impediments to the development of an Irish multi-culturalism may soon help to enable it.

Let us develop the latter point just a little. Central to the Christian faith is the conviction that this world is not our true home and that we are all nomads passing through it. Early Christianity emphasised the vital importance of offering lodging to those in exile, for they might be a chosen people. The history of the Irish, themselves dispossessed yet ever more sure of their communal identity, seemed to bear out the idea of a nation open to endless joiners: for as the Book of Leviticus taught: 'love him as yourself — for you were once strangers in Egypt' (19:33–4). What is romantic in Christianity is its openness to the notion of the Other: Jesus taught each man to love his neighbour as himself. Julia Kristeva has commented that, 'The idea of a chosen people at once defines a rational entity and implies its eternal openness — as aliens.' Of course, even that liberal Christianity too often had its own set limits: the Other was put in the place of the loved self only if he or she was a Christian.

Nonetheless, the basic implication was profound: if you are cruel to another, it must be because you are taking revenge on some hated aspect of yourself. The fear of hybridisation is really a terror in the face of potent but repressed forces within one's own culture. James Baldwin remarked many years ago of his fellow-Americans that at the root of the white man's inability to live at peace with the negro was his prior inability to live at peace with himself. It's a point worth applying more generally to humankind. The attacks by English soccer hooligans on foreign fans may well have roots in a sense of jeopardised identity, consequent upon the fact that for two centuries Englishness has been drained of much of its content to make way for Britishness. Whenever English fans were up against other groups who knew who they were, they seemed to react badly. Equally, when some German racists have burned out Turkish guest-workers, that may have been a murderous distress signal emitted by people who have turned their backs on their own traditional culture (a turning away which was in some senses understandable, given what some elements of that culture had led to).

In the United States today multi-culturalism has posed a problem. It is presented as an ideal to various recently-arrived peoples (Hispanics, Africans, Eastern Europeans) who have no sense of a common American culture, and who thus become obsessed with the identity politics of their own ethnic group, leading to that 'fraying of America' about which Arthur Schlesinger Jr has written. The old secular republican ideal, as evolved in the American Revolution, should provide the tissue uniting all, but seems no longer to do so. One manifestation of that failure is the evolving multicultural syllabus, which may in some ways serve as a warning of how *not* to do multi-culturalism in modern Ireland. This is one which presents students with entirely separate versions of Hispanic, African or Indian cultures, each of them honourably rendered in some of its richness, but none of them shown in interaction. Like the admissions policy of modern states, the admissions policy to the syllabus is also passing strange: texts are admitted single file, so to speak. Texts by black or native American authors which offer interesting accounts of their culture from within are welcomed, but there is less engagement with texts (like the poetry of Langston Hughes) which show how effectively black culture has challenged and been challenged by other traditions. The activity of the migrant worker, who challenges one sexual, religious or ethnic code with another, has been replicated in great literary works like Alice Walker's *The Color Purple*, which mingle traditional genres (slave narrative, epistolary novel, travel romance) to create brilliant new forms. This is the benefit of a necessarily messy, disputatious, promiscuous multi-culturalism, or what Stuart Hall has pithily called 'a multiculturalism without guarantees'.

Irish teachers are likely to support a multi-cultural syllabus. They may then find themselves confronted with the same challenge which faced their American counterparts — the further reduction of subventions from government to colleges on the grounds that they are harbourers of 'tenured radicals'. The perception has grown among conservative politicians in the United States that many left-wing dissidents in the 1960s, having failed to transform their society along the lines proposed by the student movement of 1968, opted instead for the lesser aim of transforming universities into 'red bases'. The emergence of courses in women's studies, postcolonial theory and popular culture is routinely described as a breach of traditional pieties and blamed on ideologically-driven teachers who are more interested in radicalising students than in studying the great minds of western culture. As Irish politics grows more American in style and theme, it is possible that right-wing politicians will seek to justify the current low level of investment in universities, in much the same way as they appear to justify the low funding for the national broadcasting station.

One of the mysteries of modern Irish politics has been the fact that politicians, ordinarily compassionate on most questions, seem determined to underfund such traditional public institutions as hospitals, despite the massive overflow of expected cash in the state's coffers. This underfunding is not as yet a conscious response to the still small numbers of immigrants arriving — but it may in time give rise to a perception among Irish people that, if recession should return, they will have to compete with many immigrants for the paltry services available.

Many politicians seem to fear 'floods', 'invasions', 'swamps' of immigrants (the language always suggests a loss of control) and they invoke 'clearance centres' as an antidote. Yet one also gets the sense that there are real divisions of opinion. The editorials of *The Sunday Business Post* (hardly a left-wing paper) repeatedly call on government to provide efficient, humane facilities for immigrants and asylum-seekers, on the grounds that our economy needs all hands to the pumps. One may assume that within Fianna Fáil there is a liberal wing, epitomised by David Andrews or Tom Kitt, which is somewhat embarrassed by all their colleagues' talk of 'flotels' and so on. It is past time for such politicians to take a more active role in debate, pointing out just how much each newly arrived person can contribute to making Ireland a better place for everyone. The old theory that the unemployed secretly gloried in their own idleness has been exploded by the willingness with which people went back to work when work materialised: and the same will be true of immigrants, who will want to augment rather than drain the public purse as soon as they can. Such people will bring with them all kinds of unseen benefits — for example, new kinds of medical therapy and holistic practices which will greatly enrich the local medical lore.

The more liberal politicians in the two main parties have remained rather quiet for their own reasons. All around them they see signs of a materialist individualism which seems to mimic that of British yob culture. The Christian churches, which might have provided a powerful moral crusade against selfishness and racism, have lost much of their teaching power and authority, and the politicians know that theirs is now in danger of a similar decline. If the belief of over 50 per cent of the public in the integrity of our system were to collapse, the country (small though it is) could disintegrate into various discrete groups, each proclaiming its moral superiority and clinging to victim status. Already, such groups as the teachers, nurses, taxi-drivers, clergy and even doctors have emitted distress signals, with farmers and the self-employed joining stay-at-home spouses in voicing deep alienation from recent trends in government policy. The insecurities of such groups are often fanned by writers in the tabloid media and few of these writers appear to invest much importance in the ideal of the republic as a guarantor of civil rights. Racism is often born of a search for scapegoats and is more likely to emerge in a climate of scapegoating, such as that promoted in scare journalism about asylum-seekers sponging on the state. Politicians, now on the defensive, are wary of espousing what might seem to be an unpopular cause.

Yet they should proceed bravely on the basis that the great majority of Irish people are not incipient or overt racists. They should support the editors of *The Irish Times* and *The Sunday Business Post* in seeking to explain why the accession of even more people may lead to even more business success. The unspoken but popular fear is that the current affluence, like sunny weather, 'will never last' and that, when it goes, the hungry immigrants will remain. Ordinary people who, at a time of affluence, see long waiting lists for basic medical care are worried that more Nigerians and Romanians will merely lengthen the queues. It is up to leaders to lead and show why the prosperity is deep-rooted — and one way of stilling those fears is to provide proper medical services.

The arguments for embracing immigrants are not just moral or cultural, but economic as well. At present the Irish labour force is seriously short of skilled and unskilled workers, and the government is in fact advertising for workers in countries like France and Spain. Those who come to Ireland in this way are here to work, and not to live on the state; and they will invariably pay far more in taxes than they will receive in state hand-outs. By tradition, it is the energetic and enterprising people from the poorer countries who usually get up and travel to another land: and the money which they earn in the host country helps, through the subventions which they send home, to reduce poverty in their native countries as well. The Irish, many of whom lived on remittance letters from Britain and the United States in the nineteenth century, should understand this better than most. So also should they recognise the immense levels of energy and creativity in those who migrate.

The fruit and vegetable harvests of the east coast over the past two years would have gone unpicked were it not for immigrant labour: and our restaurants and pubs are filled with young people from overseas who are doing work which, it seems, most of the Irish themselves no longer want. Far from depriving native workers of jobs, immigrants are doing essential work which might otherwise go undone. By their active participation in the economy, they help it to grow, creating in turn demand for other services and goods.

Nigel Harris, the main proponent of the case against immigration controls in Britain, has reminded us that there have been poor and rich countries since the beginning of time, but only in the twentieth century have controls been placed on the movement of peoples. He contends that these controls have less to do with jobs than with outmoded concepts of sovereignty — and especially with the paranoid idea that foreigners are intrinsically untrustworthy and represent at best a threat to 'our' culture and at worst a danger to the very security of the state. Harris suggests that the right to work might be separated from the right to immigrate, if states could agree to a free-flowing system in which temporary movement for work purposes (say, for one year) were possible. If the stigma of illegality were to be removed from immigrants, then many would instantly choose to work rather than be classified as refugees. A lot of them could work in those labour-intensive service industries for which there will be growing demand as the population of Europe grows more and more elderly: and, of course, as travel becomes cheaper under deregulation, many older Europeans may resettle in warmer and poorer countries, where living is cheap and the temperatures more kind.

Nigel Harris has suggested that the opening-up of borders would have the effect of increasing economic growth *worldwide*. The flow of earnings by migrant workers back to their home people would be well in excess of current aid packages for the underdeveloped world: and a truly global labour market would 'enhance welfare in both developed and developing countries'. In order to bring about these changes, he suggests the foundation of an institute like the World Trade Organisation 'to regulate movement, ensure adequate conditions for migrant workers and seek to adjust the competing interests of sending and receiving countries'. It is a bold, perhaps utopian proposal, which pays insufficient attention to the real differences in culture embedded in existing nation states and to the remarkable durability of the nation state as a formation. But it may well be that those states which can at least reduce controls on immigrants will in the longer run display the sort of flexibility and self-confidence which guarantees their survival, even in conditions of globalisation.

The fear of immigrants appears to be stronger among the old than the young. The latter don't fear losing jobs to outsiders, or losing their identity to people who might 'take Ireland away from them'. They have grown up seeing more and more black persons not just on television but in the streets. Most of today's primary schoolchildren seem quite unaware of skin colour. When they grow a little older, most of them enjoy the growing diversity of ethnic restaurants and ethnic art. And most, if asked, would vote to increase the miserly amount of overseas aid voted annually by the government, not just because it's morally right for a stronger economy to help a weaker one, but because they are shrewd enough to know that such policies will make Africa and

Asia happier places in which to live and so less likely to produce the sort of desperation that creates political refugees and economic migrants.

What these young people grasp most clearly of all is that Ireland itself was always multi-cultural, in the sense of being eclectic, open, assimilative. The best definition of a nation was that given by Joyce's Leopold Bloom: the same people living in the same place. As an outcast Jew, condemned to wandering, Bloom may in fact have had more in common with the members of the historic Irish nation than most of the characters in *Ulysses*: and he would certainly endorse the view that mono-culture works as badly in the body politic as in agriculture, rapidly wearing out the earth's potential.

Joyce wrote almost all his major texts in European exile, yet every one of them describes his native Dublin, which proved, to his satisfaction at any rate, that there is more than one way in which to live a national life. The recognition during Mary Robinson's presidency that the overseas Irish were also part of the national family suggested a corollary: that many immigrant peoples living on the island of Ireland might also have their own global communities over and above the immediate society to which they belong. In such a context, the word 'foreigner' may begin to seem a little preposterous: and that was in all probability the understanding which led Ted Turner to ban its use on CNN Global News.

When *Ulysses* headed the lists on both sides of the Atlantic as 'book of the century', Irish people everywhere felt a surge of pride, as they do when Sonia O'Sullivan wins an athletics medal. In the same spirit, following the revelations of corruption at various political tribunals, they have experienced an onset of shame. To belong to a national community is to feel personally implicated in its performance, and that is one of the moral values of such belonging. Yet there never really was a pure essence of, say, Frenchness, a fact which we all register in recognising that nations claim historic sanction and are at the same time cases of recent invention, if not instant archaeology. Nations are invariably conflations of various constituents — for instance, the Basques, Catalans, Burgundians, Provençaux and Franco-Germans all contributed to the making of modern France. Nations are in fact a response to the hybrid nature of living conditions, yet for all their claim to essential unity, they create even further hybridities. Joyce, as an early guest-worker on the continent, knew that an unprecedented knowledge is possible on the borders between cultural traditions: if *Ulysses* conflated elements of the novel, drama, lyric poem, play, opera, inventory and so on, that was to produce a wholly new genre, for which, even at the time of Joyce's own death, there was as yet no name. The central figure of that narrative, Leopold Bloom, is valued to precisely the extent that he can recognise the stranger in himself. He is, in fact, more Christ-like than any of his anti-semitic fellow-citizens and constantly able to put himself in the other fellow's position. His wife chooses him by a similar line of reasoning: 'as well him as another'.

Joyce was one of the first artists, therefore, to imagine 'a world without foreigners', a world possible once men and women begin to accept the foreigner in the self and the necessarily fictive nature of all nationalisms, which are open to endless renegotiation. He was also highly astute in locating the racist impulse in those who have an impoverished sense of history. That may seem paradoxical but isn't really: those who lack a sophisticated sense of their own origins are more likely to seek a simplified version of the past, in whose name to lash out at the 'foreign'. The other side of this dreadful coin is, of course, the sort of loathing for history disseminated by revisionists, as Julia Kristeva has explained:

> As an expression of hatred the glorification of origins finds its matching opposite in the hatred of origins. Those who repress their roots, who don't want to know where they come from, who detest their own, fuel the same hatred of self, but they think that they can settle matters by fleeing.

Kristeva goes on to assert the need for 'a nation of strangers' — one which would in turn produce a world of 'nations without nationalism'. She wishes in short to launch a critique of the idea of the nation, but without a sell-off of all its assets. If the right-wing obliterates the symbolic capital and cultural value of immigrants, she says, the left is often equally at fault in tending to question or erase the value of the national community. But without the idea of the nation, a host people can make no claim on the respect of immigrants. Those immigrants, she avers, must also honour the 'strangeness' of the culture whose sponsors welcome them in. It is worth stressing that point, because many who preach a policy of tolerance towards the cultural needs of immigrants are often the very ones who have done most to junk the claims of traditional Irish culture. Yet the national ideal has survived, for all the mockery by the media's designer

Stalinists, in rather better shape than the crude forms of Marxism in which once they believed. Millions have, rightly or wrongly, died for the nation in the past century, but nothing like those numbers have died to defend or vindicate their own social class. A national entity is, as W. B. Yeats found, a glove placed over the hand with which we reach out to hold a world: and (another happy paradox) one can never fully know one's own country or culture until one has been outside for a time and found something with which to compare them. A rich national tradition will offer its children the tools with which to critique it, just as Europe as a whole created not just colonialism but also the opposition to it, out of Hegelian dialectics.

The nation is less a legacy of the past than the site of the future, a zone of pluralisms which will prove its durability precisely by the success with which it embraces refugees, exiles and newcomers. Ireland, far from adopting a defensive policy or meekly following prescriptions from the European Union, should lead in the development of new policies. If the North/South interface between the developed and the developing worlds will be, as the Brandt Commission hinted, the key relationship in the coming century, there is a sense in which that relation has already been enacted symbolically within an Irish culture which is at once post-imperial (recognising the many Irish who helped to build the British empire) and post-colonial (aware of the great role played by those who began its dismantling).

How would this new, positive treatment of immigrants emerge? By studying the errors committed in other republics which, years before our own, tried as best their leaders could to solve these problems. Both the United States and France attempted to restrict the number of immigrants and to submit those who arrived to an Enlightenment definition of republican virtue. The result is there for all to see. In the United States, immigrants sometimes show scant respect for laws which they had no hand in framing. In France, Muslim schoolgirls are humiliatingly compelled to give up either the veil or the prospect of a state education. In both lands, the common public culture was republican, and matters of religion, cultural piety or ethnic identity were left to a purely private enactment. Congratulating itself on being neutral, the nation-state was anything but, enforcing a code of Enlightenment values on incomers. The failure of this form of 'liberal' democracy may be read in the current fraying of America and France.

The problems of Northern Ireland are relevant to this discussion. The imposition of an Enlightenment model of the state upon peoples whose traditions are very different has precluded many from full access to civic life. Put simply, under unionist domination there was no significant place within the public discourse of Northern Ireland for Catholicism or nationalism. These came to be practiced furtively, in the privacy of home or ghetto; as recently as the late 1980s few Belfast youths would have felt safe wearing a Glasgow Celtic jersey in the centre of Belfast. If the Good Friday Agreement is to thrive, Catholics must move from a time when they sought freedom from a Protestant state to one in which they seek freedom within a multi-cultural community. This process does seems to have taken a somewhat uncertain root since 1998, for all the setbacks. The emergence of such a politics carries its own ironies, given that Catholicism south of the border has become far more privatised in the same period. But the underlying issue is the same one which has arisen in the more 'advanced' states such as the French republic or welfarist Britain — the question of finding a place in the public zones for those whose religious or cultural beliefs are at variance with the codes of that secularising state which was the product of the European Enlightenment in the eighteenth century.

At the core of all societies, even bad societies, is a set of cultural codes: and nationalism has always been no more than a political and economic means by which to protect and deliver certain cultural values. There is nothing inherently wrong with any set of values being inscribed at the core of a nation state's self-designation, but this should be done in a way which encourages respect for cultural traditions. There will always be a bedrock element of civic culture to which all tax-paying citizens (and all tax-paying workers should be voting citizens) subscribe. For this to work properly in a multi-cultural society, it will be necessary to abolish the old distinction between the public sphere as the zone of reason and the private area as a place of emotion. The public sphere should now be able to project the diversity of cultures within it, rather than suppress them. In Ireland, this would involve not just showing respect for Muslims, Hindus, Jews and Buddhists, but also for Catholics and Protestants — and *that* would entail a reversal of many recent trends, which have worked to make even southern Catholicism a matter more of private than public symbolism.

Everybody has a right to practise his or her own cultural or even national traditions: and in the emerging world this should be possible even for minority cultural and national traditions within larger structures. It should, for instance, be possible for schools to ensure that Hindus or Jews or Catholics have their own special periods for internal doctrinal instruction set aside, within a teaching system which also ensures a minimal academic study of the main global traditions. In her book *Liberal Nationalism*, Yael Tamir has shown how the growth of large federal structures like the European Union should help to relax the pressure on minority groups within states, ensuring recognition for all in more relaxed configurations. Far from encouraging peoples to transcend localism (as was once thought), it may sufficiently loosen structures to allow for a more ardent expression of regional identities. Tamir contends that not all nations can realistically have self-rule of a political kind but that all should have the right to cultural self-expression, a view which seems to coincide with that taken of nationalism within Northern Ireland under the Good Friday Agreement.

Tamir argues that everyone has the right to choose a national culture and that this may be more and more a choice rather than a fixed birthright. A child of Algerian parents in a French school or a child of Catholic nationalists in Northern Ireland can decide to join a national culture: and that choice is a right because

> Outside such communities they cannot develop a language and a culture, or set themselves aims. Their lives become meaningless, there is no substance to their reflection . . . A right to culture thus entails a right to a public sphere in which individuals can share a language, memorise their past, cherish their heroes, and live a fulfilling national life.

The removal of Catholicism from the public sphere, rather than the existence of the northern state as such, was therefore the primary sin of a triumphalist unionism. This right to practise one's own culture in public should go very deep, but it can never be absolute in cases where it may override the rights of others. However, the wearing of a veil by a schoolgirl, or indeed of a turban by a motorcyclist, can hardly be said to infringe others' rights. A country whose political system works on a principle of proportional representation is in a good position to recognise and amplify all the traditions within it. And a people who have already endorsed the notions of hybridity coded into the Good Friday Agreement should have no difficulty in recognising identity as both multiple and chosen in the modern world. Such a people should, as Tamir suggests, distinguish between the rights of refugees (who have an absolute entitlement to sanctuary) and immigrants (who must recognise a state's right to exercise some controls): but they would also, as a voluntary association, grant citizenship formally to those, born within its physical confines, who finally seek it. Identity would be tied much less to ideas of land and sovereignty and more to acts of negotiation between cultures.

Of those who voted in the Republic's May 1998 referendum on the Good Friday Agreement 94 per cent decided to endorse such a working assumption: and that is an excellent start. As Julia Kristeva says: 'By recognising the other within ourselves, we are spared detesting him in himself.' If everyone recognises her or his own strangeness, the very notion of the *foreign* dissolves, to be replaced by the *strange*. (This may be why Irish language speakers tended to call the English '*stráinséirí*' rather than '*eachtrannaigh*'.) That recognition needn't be as difficult as it might seem, for the whole object of British colonialism in Ireland through the nineteenth century was, in the word of Friedrich Engels, 'to make the Irish feel like strangers in their own country'. That ordeal is something which even the stay-at-home Irish have in common with refugees and asylum-seekers: and in a reconfigured educational system, the story of that struggle should be narrated to the incomers. Extracts from Tim Pat Coogan's recent *Wherever Green is Worn: The Story of the Irish Diaspora* would be a good start. In such discussion, of course, it might also be recognised that if the Irish have often found it difficult to feel at home in Ireland, they are entitled to express some surprise at others who seem better able to feel at home there, even as they feel some solidarity with those who do not.

The experience of exiles everywhere has much in common with the cultural strategies of the Irish over the past two centuries — the use of psychological masks for self-protection; the idea of the lost homeland as vanished paradise; the certain knowledge that one was an 'other' to a host people; the need in such circumstances to self-invent and to ignore parental connections (as both Wilde and Shaw did in London); the inventive use of a new language by those who have no superstitious investment in its received protocols. If the migrant is a sign of the modern, then the Irish were modern earlier than most peoples, enduring the fate of uprooting, of learning a new language, of leaving a neolithic civilisation and settling in modern conurbations. Even those people who have moved from country to city in the past two generations have an experience which gives them something in common with that of immigrants.

The fear of the outsider is often a version of the fear of the future — for instance, those middle-Americans who interned Asians during the Second World War may have subliminally anticipated that the children of the jailed immigrants would become the prize students of science and technology at American colleges in the next two generations. In the fast-changing world of the future, a world filled with travel and resettlement, we are all likely to feel like foreigners not just at home but overseas too. Like Swift's Gulliver, we shall all find ourselves using other places as a way of analysing and improving our own, based on the understanding that our own society is the one we can reform without destroying.

Artists have traditionally asked people to recognise their own 'otherness', to understand whatever is repressed in the subconscious. Beckett took this more literally than most, producing many of his masterpieces in a second language. The French have as little difficulty as the Irish in claiming Beckett as one of their own: and his achievement is to have recognised that hatred of the other is often rooted in some prior wrong done to the other, who is punished a second time for simply reminding the unjust of their own guilt. This may well explain some of the maltreatment of immigrants from former colonies in countries like France or England, but it should cause fewer problems in Ireland. However, the fear of the foreign as a fear of what people have been schooled to repress in themselves may cause some difficulty. At the most rudimentary level, the presence of black Africans in the streets of Dublin is a reminder of a colonial past of shame and shared humiliation which some might prefer to ignore. Yet even in that painful challenge, the new immigrants are providing a priceless service, reconnecting people with their own buried feelings.

George Bernard Shaw once described himself as a sojourner on earth. That state in which everyone is open to his or her own strangeness seems a good basis on which to build a cultural democracy, which calls for respect for its own products even as it offers a similar tenderness to newcomers. Once one recognises the 'other' within the self, one has begun to engage with the thinking of the Good Friday Agreement, for as Kristeva has written:

> We must live with different people while relying on our personal moral codes, without the assistance of a set that would include our particularities while transcending them. A paradoxical community is emerging, made up of foreigners who are reconciled with themselves to the extent that they regard themselves as foreigners.

The problem is one that faces every country, not just Ireland: how to create a true multi-culturalism without levelling everything or redrawing borders between what is permissible and impermissible at some other point. The need is to create a civic nationalism. Like Irish immigrants in nineteenth-century England or the United States, many Muslims today take on the protective coloration of modernity, while continuing to practice their religious rituals in their own communities. The challenge is to build a real connection between these disparate existences, so that groups will not seek freedom *from* a secular society so much as freedom *in* a multi-cultural endeavour. The Irish in England, to be honest about it, never really solved that problem, but were simply assimilated.

Given the low levels of population growth in most European countries, it is inevitable that a shortage of labour will create a demand for immigration over coming decades. It is important that universities offer multi-cultural study courses, not alone to service members of these communities, but also to enlighten those who will deal with them. Faced with such wide choices, students are more likely to admire and endorse those codes which allow for a self-critique, rather than those which begin with the assumption that their law should prevail over all others.

At the time of writing only 500 applicants have received asylum status in Ireland. Thousands still wait to hear of their fate. In that period of uncertainty, they are prevented from taking jobs and are instead subject to 'direct provision', supplied with accommodation, food and £15 spending money per week. The identification of asylum-seekers with possible criminality feeds the assumption that many are bogus. Given the need of the economy for workers, that is a pity. The Minister for Justice, John O'Donoghue, has said that racism threatens to become a major illness of our society. While only a minority of people are abusive to non-nationals, they are having a disproportionate influence on the social climate. If politicians gave a lead in outlining the benefits brought by immigrants, ugly incidents could be much reduced in number: and if members of society were generally more willing to intervene in cases of assault and attack, the number of violent acts would drop further still. The evil of racism is a subset of an even wider problem: the collapse of respect for *res publica*, the loss of faith in society as such. Such a faith can only be restored if leaders outline a national philosophy and not just programmes of economic self-interest. For the ultimate paradox is this: that only a people secure in their national philosophy are capable of dealing confidently with those who come among them with deep commitments to alternative codes.

Bibliographies

Multi-culturalism and Northern Ireland: Edna Longley

Boal, Frederick W. et al., *Them and Us: Attitudinal Variations Among Church-goers in Belfast* (Institute of Irish Studies, Queen's University Belfast, 1997)

Bloomfield, Sir Kenneth, *We Will Remember Them: The Report of the Northern Ireland Victims Commissioner* (1998)

Butler, Hubert, *Escape from the Anthill* (Lilliput Press, 1985), *Grandmother and Wolfe Tone* (Lilliput Press, 1990)

Catalyst publications, such as Johnston McMaster's *Churches on the Edge*, can be obtained from Norman Gibson, 39 Glenbroome Park, Newtownabbey, Co. Antrim BT37 0RL

Colley, Linda, *Britons: Forging the Nation 1707-1837* (Yale University Press, 1992)

Crozier, Maurna (ed.), *Varieties of Irishness* (Institute of Irish Studies, 1989)

Dunlop, John, *A Precarious Belonging: Presbyterians and the Conflict in Ireland* (Blackstaff Press, 1995)

ECONI publications can be obtained from ECONI, 12 Wellington Place, Belfast BT1 6GE

Elliott, Marianne, *The Catholics of Ulster: A History* (Allen Lane: The Penguin Press, 2000)

Faith and Politics Group, *Doing Unto Others: Parity of Esteem in a Contested Space* (Faith and Politics Group, 8 Upper Crescent, Belfast BT7 1NT, 1997)

Farren, Sean, *The Politics of Irish Education 1920-65* (Institute of Irish Studies, 1995)

Holmes, David G., 'The Eucharistic Congress of 1932 and Irish Identity', *New Hibernia Review* 4, 1 (Spring 2000)

Irish Inter-Church Meeting, *Sectarianism: A Discussion Document* (1993)

Ignatieff, Michael, *Blood and Belonging: Journeys into the New Nationalism* (Farrar, Straus and Giroux, 1994)

Kirk, John, 'Ulster Scots: Realities and Myths', *Ulster Folklife,* Vol. 44 (1998)

Leonard, Jane, *Memorials to the Casualties of Conflict: Northern Ireland 1969 to 1997* (Community Relations Council, 1997)

Logue, Paddy (ed.), *Being Irish: Personal Reflections on Irish Identity Today* (Oak Tree Press, 2000)

Lucy, Gordon and Elaine McClure (eds), *Remembrance* (Ulster Society, 1997)

McCoy, Gordon with Maolcholaim Scott, *Gaelic Identities* (Institute of Irish Studies, 2000)

McIntosh, Gillian, *The Force of Culture: Unionist Identities in Twentieth-Century Ireland* (Cork University Press, 1999)

McKay, Susan, *Northern Protestants: An Unsettled People* (Blackstaff Press, 2000)

McKittrick, David, Seamus Kelters, Brian Feeney, Chris Thornton, *Lost Lives: The Stories of the Men, Women and Children who Died as a Result of the Northern Ireland Troubles* (Mainstream, 1999)

MacLachlan, Malcolm and Michael O'Connell, *Cultivating Pluralism* (Oak Tree Press, 2000)

Mac Póilin, Aodán, 'Language, Identity and Politics in Northern Ireland', *Ulster Folklife*, Vol. 45 (1999)

Morgan, Michael, 'Dinosaurs and Frankensteins', *Fortnight* 389 (November 2000)

Morrow, Duncan, *'It's Not Everyone You Could Tell That To'* (Northern Ireland Community Relations Council, 1997)

O'Connor, Fionnuala, *In Search of a State: Catholics in Northern Ireland* (Blackstaff Press, 1993)

O'Doherty, Malachi, *The Trouble with Guns: Republican Strategy and the Provisional IRA* (Blackstaff Press, 1998)

Ryan, Ray (ed.), *Writing in the Irish Republic: Literature, Culture, Politics 1949-1999* (Macmillan, 2000)

Wilson, Robin, 'The Politics of Contemporary Ethno-Nationalist Conflicts', unpublished article

Strangers in their Own Country: Declan Kiberd

Caldwell, June, 'Are We Becoming a Nation of Racists?' *Woman's Way*, Vol. 38, No. 37, 22 September 2000

Coulter, Carol, 'Courts to Face More Challenges on Asylum Question', *The Irish Times*, 29 August 2000

Handlin, Oscar, *Old Boston* (1989)

Harris, Nigel, 'Should Europe End Immigration Controls? A Polemic', *European Journal of Development Research*, Vol. 12, No. 1, June 2000

Hughes, Robert, *The Culture of Complaint* (Oxford University Press), 1993

Kiberd, Declan, 'Reinventing England', *Keywords: A Journal of Cultural Materialism*, 2, 1999

Kristeva, Julia, *Strangers to Ourselves*, transl. Leon S. Roudiez (Harvester Wheatsheaf, 1991)

___ *Nations Without Nationalism*, transl. Leon S. Roudiez (Columbia University Press, 1993)

Nairn, Tom, *Faces of Nationalism* (Verso, 1997)

Nelson, Cary, *Memoirs of a Tenured Radical* (1997)

Schmuhl, Robert, *Indecent Liberties* (2000)

Tamir, Yael, *Liberal Nationalism* (Princeton, 1993)